62 Tax Dodges - Safe, Effective Ways to Pay Less Tax

THE COMPLEMENTARY WEBSITE

The http://books.indicator.co.uk website gives you instant access to all the ready-to-use documents, tools, policies, etc. that complement this publication.

Go to

http://books.indicator.co.uk

and enter your access code
BUT929

THE CD-ROM

Don't have access to the Internet?
Call Customer Services on 01233 653500 to request a CD-ROM.

Indicator

Cover: ©iStockphoto.com

Second Edition - First Print - E02P1

ISBN 978-1-906892-53-1

Introduction

The key to keeping your tax bill down is understanding how the system works and knowing where the loopholes are. But you probably don't have the time or the will to get to grips with the countless long-winded and tricky rules published by the Taxman. What you need is advice from a tax expert, but this doesn't come cheap. That's why we've put together 62 of our top tax dodges in one book. They're all bang up-to-date and cover almost every angle of tax from personal income to capital and company taxes.

The book is divided into sections each relating to a different topic, e.g. remuneration and Inheritance Tax, making it easy to find what you're looking for. "62 Tax Dodges - Safe, Effective Ways to Pay Less Tax" offers you expert tax-saving advice at a fraction of the normal cost. So don't miss out on this chance to start cutting your tax bill now.

Tony Court
June 2012

Table of contents

Section 1 - Cars

Section 2 - Capital Gains Tax

Section 3 - Corporation Tax

Section 9 - Property

Section 10 - Remuneration

Section 11 - Appendices

SECTION 1

Cars

One of the most asked tax questions is whether it's a good idea to have a company car or not. Whilst there's no right answer, as each case depends on many different factors, there are ways you can save tax.

Whether it's choosing the right make and model to keep your tax bill down, or how to make tax-free cash from selling your car to your company, this section gives you pointers on how to do it.

1. The classic car solution

Problem

The costs of running and maintaining a classic car can be high. However, where your company owns the vehicle, it can claim these costs against its Corporation Tax bill, but this will mean a tax charge for you under the benefit-in-kind (BiK) rules. How can you minimise this?

What counts as a classic car?

The Taxman defines classic cars as those that are:

- at least 15 years old (from the original date of registration); and
- have a market value of at least £15,000. Such vehicles are taxed on their market value.

However, the definition of a tax-efficient classic car is one that is more than 15 years old but whose current market value is less than £15,000. For example, a 1963 MGB Roadster that originally cost £500 which now has a market value of £8,000.

How much tax?

Company cars, apart from certain exemptions, are subject to a BiK tax charge based on the CO_2 emissions rating of the car together with its original list price. However, most classic cars don't have an emissions rating and so an alternative method of calculating the BiK must be used.

The percentage of list price used to calculate the benefit will instead be based on the engine size: less than 1,400cc - 15%; between 1,400cc and 2,000cc - 25%; and more than 2,000cc - 35%. For example, the MGB roadster has a 1,600cc engine so the benefit is 25% of list price.

However, it's the original list price that you use, not the classic car's current market value. The MGB roadster only cost £500 back in 1963 so the taxable benefit is just 25% of this figure, i.e. £125 (£500 x 25%). As a 50% taxpayer your income tax bill is only £62.50 (£125 x 50%) and the company pays employers' Class 1A NI of £17.25 (£125 x 13.8%).

TIP

As a "classic" company car choose one that's worth less than £15,000 with a low (in current prices) original list price. This way you drive down the tax cost of having it owned by the company. Meanwhile, you get the company to pay for all the repair bills.

TIP

Don't let the company pay for fuel you use for private motoring as this brings an automatic BiK charge calculated by applying the car benefit percentage to a fixed figure (£21,200 for 2012/13). In our example of the MGB Roadster, that's 25% of £18,000, resulting in £5,300 taxable benefit.

Age and value warning

If your classic car is worth more than £15,000 at the beginning of a next tax year and is also more than 15 years old on that date, the taxable benefit is calculated on its market value rather than the original price. Keep an eye on the car's market value to make sure you don't get a nasty tax surprise.

Added accessories

Any significant accessories you add to the car which were not included in its original specification, such as an audio system, must be added to the list price in the taxable benefit calculation. This will mean more tax to pay. But money spent on a repair or replacement of a worn out original accessory etc. won't affect the tax charge.

Solution

Taxable car benefit is worked out from the original price of a classic car where it's worth less than £15,000. For example, with an original cost of £500, your tax bill is only £50; plus, the company picks up the tab for the running costs.

2. Tax breaks for environmentally friendly cars

Problem

Two sets of calculations are needed to work out the true cost of tax and NI on a company car; one for your company and the other for the director or employee who drives the car. These calculations used to be based on entirely different data but now they are both linked to the car's environmental impact. How do you work out the most tax-efficient vehicle for you and your business?

Capital allowances

In April 2009 the rate at which your company could claim capital allowances (CAs), i.e. the Taxman's version of depreciation, changed from being based on price to being linked to CO_2 emissions. For cars with CO_2 emissions over 160g/km, you can claim CAs equal to just 8% (from April 2012) of the cost of the car each year on a reducing balance. But for those producing less CO_2, you'll get CAs at the rate of 18% (from April 2012). Even if you sell the car after a few years, the tax relief just trickles along at these same rates.

Reducing tax relief

The differential in the CA rates mean that you should aim to buy cars which have emissions below 160g/km. After five years you will have received tax relief of around 61% of the cost, compared to just 34% for cars with higher CO_2 emissions. With these ever dwindling rates of relief it's an opportune time to take a closer look at the tax breaks for company cars.

Ultra low CO_2

There is a way that you can forget about spreading tax relief over a number of years.

TIP

There's a very low emissions limit of 110g/km. Where your company buys a car which has emissions at this level or lower, you can claim 100% of the cost against tax for the year of purchase. And if you're talking about cars for several employees, this accelerated tax relief can really mount up.

Choice of car

Most people probably think that neither you nor your employees would want to be driving around in a Smart car just to earn this tax break. But actually cars like the Audi A3, BMW 320d or the Honda Civic, to name just a few, also fall in to the sub-111g/km bracket. (For weblinks to check the types of vehicle that are on offer see Appendix.)

Savings for the user

It's not just CAs where tax can be saved. The benefit-in-kind for those driving the car decreases in line with the CO_2 emissions. And for the same reason so will the NI your company has to pay. Even if you don't fancy one of the very low CO_2 emission cars for yourself, it's now time to rethink what you offer your staff; it could save your company thousands of pounds.

Solution

If you want the most tax-efficient company cars, buy those with CO_2 emissions below 111g/km. You can claim the full cost as a tax deduction for the year of purchase, and the benefit-in-kind on which tax and NI is based will also be lower.

3. Accessorising your company car

Problem

The amount of tax payable on company cars is calculated from a combination of how much CO_2 the vehicle emits, together with its original list price. The higher the emissions, the greater the percentage of the list price is taxed, and this must include the cost of any extras fitted, such as a sat nav. How can you reduce the tax on these?

Example

James decides his four-year-old car needs replacing. He's looking at a similar model costing £20,000 with CO_2 emissions of 200g/km. The taxable benefit is 3% of the list price which amounts to £6,000. But James decides to treat himself to the manufacturer's fitted "entertainment pack". This adds £2,000 to the list price and another £600 to the taxable benefit (£2,000 x 30%).

Exemptions

The Taxman won't charge tax on extras with a list price totalling £100 or less, but that's not going to get you much these days. However, there's an exemption that's often overlooked. There's no tax on extras if they're to be used for the business. The Taxman gives an example of a tow-bar that's used to pull a trailer for carrying equipment.

TIP

If your job means that you drive to many different locations, it's fair to say that a sat nav could be used for this. It can therefore be excluded from the benefit-in-kind (BiK) tax charge.

TIP

Make sure that whoever is preparing your Forms P11D (end of year benefits and expenses return) is aware of any extras that need to be excluded from the list price of the car.

Detachable benefits

It's difficult to justify a tax exemption for a DVD player as an extra on the basis that it's necessary for your business. But even if you can't avoid a tax charge, there is a way you can reduce the amount payable. The cost of extras is only added to the list price of the car if they are fixed to the vehicle. So a DVD player, or any other accessory that isn't fitted to the car, won't be charged to tax under the same rules. Instead, the BiK is calculated at a flat rate of 20% of the cost of the extra.

Example

Assume the same facts as the example above, but instead of adding the manufacturer's options James purchases separate DVD and sat nav systems that are detachable. These cost him the same amount as the built-in ones - £2,000. But he'll now pay tax only on a BiK of £400 (£2,000 x 20%).

Trap. Some cars have a BiK rate of less than 20%. If this is the case, then adding fitted extras will cost less in tax than detachable versions.

TIP

The tax payable on a detachable extra for your car is based on what your company pays for it, rather than the original list price. That's useful in today's market because there are some good discounts to be had if you shop around.

What about NI?

Employers' NI contributions are due on BiKs at 13.8%. So if you can reduce the BiK charge on a car accessory, not only will you save tax, but your company can also cut its NI costs.

Solution

You can avoid paying tax on car accessories, such as a sat nav, by making sure you use it at least occasionally for business. But where business use is not possible, you can reduce the tax and NI bill by buying a detachable version.

4.   Selling a car to your company

Problem

The taxable benefit-in-kind (BiK) for the private use of a company car is calculated according to CO_2 emissions rather than linking it to business mileage or the number of company vehicles. How can you take advantage?

Tax-free cash for your car

If you already have a company car but own a second one privately, you can sell it to your company at its market value. Where the company then lets you use the car for private motoring, you will have to pay tax on it as a BiK, but the company will be able to claim tax relief on the cost of buying the car from you and all the future running costs.

Example

Let's say that your company already provides your main car and your partner drives one that's privately owned and is about 15 months old. Its list price when new was £10,000 and it has CO_2 emissions of 149g/km. You sell it to your company for its current second-hand value of £8,000. The average running costs, e.g. insurance, maintenance, NI etc., come to approximately £1,000 a year. The tax you will pay, assuming you're liable at 40%, is £800 per year, or £400 if you are only a basic rate payer. The company will also get tax relief worth at least £750. (For a more detailed example see the Appendix.)

The annual tax charges you will pay and tax relief the company will get are very nearly equal. But the company now owns an asset worth £8,000, and you have the same amount of cash in your bank account tax-free

> **TIP**
>
> This idea works just as well even if the car you sell is your only one. But the reason this two-car scheme is interesting is that it's now tax efficient. Until several years ago the tax charge was increased by 50% if you had more than one company car. So selling your second car to the company and getting it back as a BiK would have created a disproportionate tax bill. But now there is no additional charge no matter how many company cars you have.

Trap. If the car is subject to a finance agreement such as hire purchase (HP), you'll probably need permission from the HP company before you sell it. So you must make sure you check the small print on your contract first.

TIP

If an HP, or similar, contract doesn't permit you to sell the car, your company could lend you the money to pay off the contract. Then when you sell the car to your company, you can use the proceeds you receive to repay the money you borrowed. Any BiK charge for the beneficial loan would be negligible as the borrowing should only be for a matter of days.

Trap. There's no point trying this scheme with an old banger as you won't be able to get enough money for the car from your company to make the scheme work. This is because the BiK tax on cars is based on their original list price not what they are worth now. So you are likely to end up with little money and a high tax bill.

Solution

Extract a tax-free payment from your company by selling it your privately owned car. You can continue to use it, although this will result in a tax charge under the BiK rules. The charge will be based on its original list price, so don't try this scheme with an old vehicle that's not worth much.

5.   Tax deduction for privately owned cars

Problem

Tax relief on buying a car for your business is given a little at a time in the form of depreciation, known as a capital allowance (CA). For cars bought after April 6 2009 (April 1 for companies) you will have to wait over 20 years to get the tax relief you're entitled to. How can you speed up the process?

Tax deductions

For cars with CO_2 emissions exceeding 160g/km, you are allowed to claim CAs equal to 8% (from April 2012) of their cost in the year of purchase. The remaining 90% is carried forward and 10% of this amount is allowed as a CA in the following year. The reduced balance is carried forward again, and so on. A similar principle is applied to cars with CO_2 emissions of less than 160g/km but the CA rate in that case is 18% (from April 2012) per annum.

Car pooling

The cost of all cars bought by a business is grouped together in either a 8% or 18% "pool" of expenditure. CAs continue at just 8% or 18% of the reducing pool value even after the car is sold. This means full tax relief takes over two decades to achieve. But there is a loophole that can speed things up, although currently this can only be used by the self-employed or those in partnership.

If there is any private use of a car, the CA rules say that the value can't be pooled. So when the car is sold any cost that hasn't been allowed for tax by claiming the 8% or 18% CA, will be given in full in the year of sale. This final chunk of tax relief is called a "balancing allowance".

Private use - the bad news

Although the private use of a car or asset will accelerate tax relief, it also means that the amount you can claim will be reduced.

Example

Bob is self-employed as a consultant. He bought a car in May 2011 for £20,000. It has CO_2 emissions of 200g/km. He uses it for business 80% of the time and the remainder is private use. The CAs he can claim on the car are restricted in proportion to his business use so that in the year of purchase he'll get CAs of £1,280 (£20,000 x 10% x 80%). When he sells the car he can claim a CA, but that will also be restricted to the 80% business use element.

The CA rules say that cars you provide to your employees must always be included in either the 8% or 18% pool subject to the CO_2 emissions. But there is a way you can use the private use rule to change this.

Solution

Build into your company car policy a requirement that your employees must give up their car for use by the business owner or partner if required. Obviously you'll need to co-ordinate with your employee to avoid problems, but it shouldn't be too difficult to find genuine reasons to use their car, say when yours is in for service or repair, your spouse needs to use a car, going to the shops during the working day, or taking clients out for a business lunch, etc.

Keep a record of your private mileage. Aim to use the car this way for about 5% of the total miles it covers in a year. That way the restriction will be minimal and outweighed by the cash flow advantage of getting your tax relief much sooner.

SECTION 2

Capital Gains Tax

In 2008 the rate of Capital Gains Tax was radically reduced from a 40% maximum to a fixed 18%. But in June 2010 an additional Capital Gains Tax rate of 28% was added for higher rate taxpayers making it more important to find ways to avoid this.

From maximising your annual exemptions to using family gifts, this section offers you a range of tax dodges aimed at cutting your Capital Gains Tax bill.

6.   Gift of a holiday home

Problem

You want to pass on your second home to your children as part of an Inheritance Tax planning exercise, but there's likely to be a large Capital Gains Tax bill to pay. How can you avoid this?

Tax and gifts of assets

Passing on your assets during your lifetime generally reduces the value of your estate which is subject to Inheritance Tax (IHT), meaning less tax is payable on your death. The value of the gift made to an individual will drop out of your estate completely once you have lived seven years from the date you made it.

Capital Gains Tax trap

Unfortunately, for Capital Gains Tax (CGT) purposes the transfer of a property to a relative who is not your spouse is taxed as if you had sold it at the full market value. And where it's increased in value, you might have tax to pay on the profit you make.

Use a trust

One solution is to transfer the property to a discretionary trust set up to benefit your children. The value of such a gift is potentially subject to IHT; it won't actually be exempt until seven years has passed from the time of the gift. Also, the capital gain (profit) on the property is subject to CGT.

To avoid this potential double taxation you can elect, under s.260 of the **Taxation of Capital Gains Act 1992** (TCGA), to "hold over" the CGT which leaves none to pay on the gift. There's also no IHT to pay if the value of the property is less than your unused nil-rate band for IHT (£325,000 until April 2015).

When the property is eventually sold all of the gain built up when it was in your hands is taxable, as well as any increase in value achieved since the date of the gift.

Property rental alternative

If the property is classed as a business asset, you can gift it directly to your children and hold over the capital gain under s.165 of TCGA. Business assets include properties that have been let commercially as furnished holiday lettings.

TIP

Where you have a second home which you would like to pass on to your children free of tax, let it out furnished for a few seasons to meet the furnished holiday let conditions (see Appendix).

Once it qualifies as a business asset, and you've transferred it to your offspring, they can occupy it and claim the CGT exemption for living in the property as their main home. This means the gains that built up on the property while it was in your hands have escaped tax completely. The gains made since the date of the gift are exempt due to the main residence exemption.

Solution

Rent out the property as a furnished holiday let for a few seasons to establish a valid business under the Taxman's rules. This means when it's given away to one of your children there's no immediate CGT bill.

7. Using capital losses against your income tax bill

Problem

Where you lose money on shares which you subscribed for in an unquoted company (this might be your own company), you can set these against capital gains you make from the sale of any other assets. But the maximum rate of tax relief you can achieve is 28%. How can you increase the rate of tax relief to up to 50%?

CGT v income tax rates

Despite the introduction of a higher Capital Gains Tax (CGT) rate from June 2010 of 28%, it remains much lower than the top rate of income tax of 50%. This disparity has led tax experts to look for ways of converting income into gains to benefit from the lower rate.

Turning income into gains

Turning income into gains is a good tax strategy but difficult to achieve. On the other hand, it makes just as much sense to take a capital loss, which can usually be used only to reduce CGT payable at 28%, and set it against income chargeable at rates of up to 50%. For example, a capital loss made in 2010/11 can be set against capital gains made in the same year. Or in some cases you can carry it forward to set against gains of later years. Either way, the maximum rate of tax saving is 28%. But certain capital losses can be set against your income tax bill and so get you income tax relief at 50%.

Capital to income

If you've subscribed for shares, i.e. bought them directly from a company, and it's an unquoted trading company, then subject to a few other conditions, any loss you make on the shares can be converted from a CGT loss into one that you can set against your income. (For a weblink to the Taxman's website on the conditions see the Appendix).

Example

James is a higher rate taxpayer with total income of around £115,000. He bought 5,000 shares in Smallco Ltd for £15,000 in 2004. The share value has dropped to £1 each, leaving him with an overall loss of £10,000 on paper. James decides to cut his losses and sell the shares in February 2013. He can set the resulting loss against current or future capital gains and get maximum tax relief of £2,800. Or instead he can make an election to set the loss against his income tax and get tax relief worth £5,000 (£10,000 x 50%).

TIP

At the risk of the shares devaluing further, James could wait to sell them until after April 5 2013. By doing so he can claim the loss against next year's income. Because of the hike in tax rates, he'll boost his tax relief up to £6,000 (£10,000 x 60%).

Download Zone

For a free sample **Draft Election**, visit **http://books.indicator.co.uk**. You'll find the access code on page 2 of this book.

TIP

If James wants to hang on to his shares in Smallco, there is a way he can "have his cake and eat it". He could sell the shares creating the CGT loss to set against his income, and then buy them back, provided he allows 30 days to elapse between the sale contract date and the repurchase.

Solution

Elect for losses you make from selling shares in unquoted trading companies to be set against your income tax liability. This will increase the tax relief from 28% to a maximum of 50%.

8. Tax and marriage breakdowns

Problem

The last thing on your mind when you are going through a divorce will probably be the tax consequences, but ignoring the effect on your Capital Gains Tax could prove expensive.

Background

Married couples hopefully build up substantial value in assets together, ranging from bank accounts to houses. When these are divided at the end of a marriage there could be tax consequences.

Example

Some years before their marriage ended Mr A bought a commercial property that he let. As part of usual tax planning wisdom he transferred a half share of the property to his wife who, having no other income, could receive her share of the rent at lower rates of tax.

They separated in August 2010, at which time the property value was nearly £200,000 more than the original cost. As part of the divorce settlement Mr A transferred his share of the property to Mrs A. They agreed to this arrangement in May 2011.

The Taxman demanded nearly £30,000 in Capital Gains Tax (CGT) saying that he deemed Mr A had sold his share of the property to Mrs A at market value, which resulted in a large capital gain even though he had not received a penny.

Transfers between married couples

Usually, transfers between a husband and wife or between those in a civil partnership are treated as taking place on a "no gain and no loss" (NGNL) basis; therefore, there are no significant tax consequences. But this only applies in a tax year during which they are living together as a couple.

Therefore, if the transfer of an asset takes place after the tax year in which they separated, but before they are divorced, then it's not dealt with on the NGNL basis.

What if no money changes hands?

Even though a couple may be separated, they are considered to be "connected persons" by the Taxman until they are divorced, i.e. the decree absolute is issued. Special anti-avoidance tax rules apply to connected persons so that, whether any money changes hands or not, any transfer of assets between them is treated as if it were a sale at full market value.

When are you separated for tax purposes?

It's vital that couples considering divorce know when in the Taxman's eyes he considers them separated:

The Taxman defines a married couple (or couple within a civil partnership) as separated if they are not living together in a full relationship, and that arrangement is likely to be a permanent one. Thus a period apart only intended to be a temporary break is not separation for tax purposes and all the special tax rules relating to married couples and those within a civil partnership still apply.

Solution

As cold and calculating as this sounds, if you and your spouse intend to separate, don't do it close to the end of the tax year, e.g. if you separate on March 31, any transfer of assets between you after April 5 but before you are divorced will be deemed to be a sale at market value.

If time is short but you know some of the assets you intend to transfer between you, agree this in a contract by the April 5 following your separation, as for CGT purposes the contract date is the date of transfer.

9.   Deferring the CGT bill on shares

Problem

Usually, when you give away some shares in your company this will result in a Capital Gains Tax (CGT) bill. How can you reduce or avoid this?

CGT problem

The rule is that the Taxman can tax any transfer of existing shares as if they had been sold at their market value (s.17(1)(a) of the **Taxation of Capital Gains Act 1992)**.

Example

Your company is worth £200,000 but you only paid £1,000 for your shares. By transferring 50% of your shares to someone else, let's call him Mr X, this will result in a gain of £99,500. If you pay tax at the higher (40%) or additional rates (50%), the CGT bill will be 28% of the gain, i.e. on transfer it will be £27,860 (£99,500 x 28%). In addition to CGT, Stamp Duty is payable; this is another £500 (£100,000 x 0.5%).

Dilute your shareholding

If CGT arises on the transfer of existing shares, instead of selling/transferring them to Mr X, get him to buy new shares in the company. And if you don't buy any of these new shares, this will dilute your total shareholding. If you have 100% of the company with 1,000 £1 shares and the company issues another 1,000 shares to someone else, you are left owning only 50% of the company.

By doing this you've not sold or given away any of your original shares to give rise to a capital gain. There is also no Stamp Duty to pay on new share issues. The Taxman will argue that you have "shifted" value away from your shareholding artificially and that the issue of shares has been made at undervalue. He will treat this as a disposal by you at market value. In our example, you are back to the £27,860 tax bill.

2

Solution

Gains resulting from the gifts of shares in an unquoted trading company aren't subject to CGT at the time of the gift where the donor and the beneficiary of the gift both sign a declaration (Form IR295) to defer taxing of this gain until the shares are sold or value paid on winding up of the company. (See the Appendix for a weblink to HMRC Help Sheet IR295.)

Step 1. Agree on the new shareholdings.

Step 2. Hold a director's meeting to approve the proposed share transfers to achieve those shareholdings. Make sure proper minutes of the meeting are drawn up by the company secretary, are approved, signed and filed with the statutory records.

Step 3. Fill out the appropriate forms; at most it's a question of ticking some boxes. Help Sheet IR295 contains the two forms (pages 6 and 7). Ignore the boxes that ask for an "asset value". Both must be signed by you and the donee.

Result. You won't be charged to tax at all and neither will the donee (until they sell/ transfer the shares). And later, if the donee does give away the shares, they too can elect to have the tax on the gain deferred.

10. Entrepreneurs' relief for employees

Problem

Entrepreneurs' relief can apply when you sell shares in your own company. However, there is a trap concerning employees that could disqualify you.

Entrepreneurs' relief

Entrepreneurs' relief (ER) can apply to gains made when you sell part or all of your business, or shares in your own company, subject to a gains cap of £5 million. The Capital Gains Tax (CGT) rate on gains to which ER applies is 10%.

Conditions for ER

To qualify for the ER tax rate you must have held the shares or business assets for at least a year before the sale, and the business must be a trading one, i.e. not for holding investments. Also you'll usually have to own 5% or more of the ordinary shares in the company.

Example

You sell the shares in your company for a gain of £450,000. ER reduces the tax due to £45,000. This can be reduced further where you haven't used your CGT annual exemption (£10,600 for 2012/13) on other gains in the year. And where you've made capital losses in earlier years, these too can be used against the CGT bill.

Officer or employee trap

To qualify for ER the shares being sold must be in the owner's personal company. The definition of which is:

- one in which the shareholder owns at least 5% of the ordinary share capital of the company, and as a result can exercise 5% of the voting rights; and
- the owner has been an officer or employee for the twelve months prior to the sale.

If the shareholder hasn't been an employee or officer in the company for the twelve months, they won't qualify for ER, so will attract CGT at 18% or 28%.

Solutions

Become an officer. Obviously, being a director would qualify as an officer of the company. And just being the company secretary would also help qualify a shareholder for ER. For example, if your spouse also holds shares but doesn't work for the company and isn't already a director, make them company secretary in order for their shareholding to qualify.

Contracts of employment. Make sure you have some form of employment relationship with the company. There is no requirement to be a full-time employee of the company, so part-time jobs or consultancy contracts with the company would suffice. Back this up with contracts of employment and by putting yourself on the payroll.

11. Company share buy back

Problem

Where you sell your shares back to your company, you can ask the Taxman to apply the Capital Gains Tax (CGT) rates instead of the less generous ones for income tax. This can save tax, but what if he refuses?

The CGT option

Where your company buys back its own shares from you, the money you receive will be taxed as if it were a dividend. This means income tax rates of up to 50% will apply. But there's an option to treat the money as if it were received from a normal sale of shares. In that case CGT will apply, meaning you can benefit from lower tax rates and extra exemptions. But there's a catch.

Clearance

The CGT option only applies where the Taxman has approved its special clearance procedure, and he won't do this unless certain conditions are met:

- the company must be an unquoted trading company or the holding company of a trading group
- the purchase should be for the benefit of the company's trade
- the purchase isn't part of a scheme to avoid tax
- the seller should be resident and ordinarily resident in the United Kingdom in the tax year of the purchase
- the shares must have been owned for at least five years before the date of the sale (three years if they were inherited)
- the seller must not retain 30% or more of the company's issued share capital of the company, or a right to acquire more than 30%
- the seller's interest in shares in the company should be substantially reduced, i.e. their holding after the repurchase should not be more than 75% before the purchase.

(For a weblink on how to apply for a clearance for CGT treatment see the Appendix.)

Trap. The Taxman has the final say on whether the last condition is met and he can be very awkward. Essentially, you have to prove that the share purchase will have a positive effect on the business.

Paying dividends instead

If CGT treatment doesn't apply, then the basic tax rule will mean that the money the company pays you for the shares is taxable as a dividend, but not all of it.

TIP

You can deduct the original cost of the shares, i.e. the amount the company received for them when they were first issued. Only the amount you receive over and above this will be taxed as if it were a dividend.

Dividend advantages

Having the money taxed as a dividend isn't all bad news, at least there won't be any NI for you or the company to pay. And there's no tax to pay at all where the dividend, along with your other taxable income, doesn't exceed the basic rate band (BRB).

TIP

Before selling the shares to the company you can give some or all of them to your spouse if they have basic rate or 40% tax bands to use up. For example, this could save you tax of nearly £10,000 where your spouse has no other income. And you can use this tip in conjunction with the one below.

TIP

Defer and spread the share sale. If the sale of the shares is linked to your retirement, after which your income will fall leaving you with some BRB to spare, you can use this to lower or completely dodge the tax. Arrange to sell the shares in chunks over several years. You'll get the same money overall but by spreading it over a number of years you'll have multiple BRBs available to you.

Solution

If the Taxman refuses to allow CGT treatment on a company share buy-back, you'll be subject to the less generous income tax rules. But you can save tax by transferring shares to your spouse before the sale to use up their tax exemption. You can also spread the share sale over several years and so benefit from multiple BRBs.

12. Reducing CGT on gifts

Problem

Gifts of assets are treated as transfers at market value. And where the market value is greater than the cost of the shares, you can be liable to a Capital Gains Tax (CGT) charge. How can you minimise this?

Transfer now

Gifts of assets are not generally free of CGT if their market value exceeds the cost to the donor.

Example

Roger wishes to give his son a rental property he has held for many years. The property was bought in 1970 for £15,000 and was worth £45,000 in March 1982. Its current value in October 2012 is estimated at £200,000. The gain is calculated as follows:

	£
Current market value	200,000
Less market value at March 31 1982	(45,000)
Gross gain	155,000
Annual exemption	(10,600)
Taxable gain	144,400
Tax at 28%	40,432

NOTE. It's assumed that Roger pays higher rate tax. If he didn't, then the part of the gain, when added to his income, which fell below the basic rate band (£34,370 for 2012/13) would be chargeable at 18%.

Would it make any difference if Roger delayed the transfer until the start of a new tax year?

Solution

If Roger is married, he could transfer a half share in the property to his wife. Both could then gift their shares to use their annual exemptions and hopefully the spouse's basic rate tax band to benefit from the 18% CGT rate.

Gifts can be spread over two or more tax years so that more than one annual exemption is utilised.

13.   CGT planning with children

Problem

There's no exemption from CGT for a property other than the one for your only or main private residence. This means you'll have to pay tax on any gain you make from selling it. How can your children play a part in reducing this?

Tax-free gains

Every individual has an annual Capital Gains Tax (CGT) exemption which, for 2012/13, is £10,600. Where you make capital gains in excess of this they are taxed at 18% or 28% depending on the level of your income. Even children under 18 years old are entitled to an annual exemption.

Anti-avoidance rules

If you give an asset to your child, the Taxman will treat this as if you sold it to them at market value. This tax "anti-avoidance" rule can actually be used in your favour.

Example

You paid £90,000 for a property in 1990, and despite the fall in the market, it's now worth £190,000. You don't want to sell it now as you think the value will improve, but the catch is that the greater the property's value, the more CGT you'll have to pay.

However, if you have two children and you can give one a tenth share in the property before April 5 2013, and the other a similar share soon after that date, you'll ultimately reduce the CGT bill. The Taxman treats both gifts as sales at market value producing a capital gain of approximately £10,000 for each, i.e. the gain on sale of whole property would be £100,000 and a gain on one tenth of it will be £10,000 (see note below). As the gains fall into two tax years, 2011/12 and 2012/13, you can use your tax-free exemption for each year to cover both gains, so there will be no tax to pay.

NOTE. In our example we've given the market value of a 10% share in a property as 10% of the full market value of the whole property. But in practice where you make a gift of a minority share in an asset, its market value is discounted. For a property, this would typically be by 15% to 20% for a 10% share. So the market value of a 10% share in a property worth £200,000 would be around £16,000.

Assume values do recover, and you sell the property in the tax year 2014/15. This will result in a capital gain for you and your children. You will each be entitled to a CGT exemption for that year, which can be used to reduce the amount chargeable to tax. Altogether, by using your children's CGT exemptions you have sheltered up to £40,000 of capital gain and saved tax of up to £10,600 (see the Appendix for the calculation).

TIP

If you transfer assets to your children, make sure you have evidence. Draw up a deed of gift and have it witnessed. If you are not sure how to do this, ask a solicitor. It shouldn't cost more than around £350 plus VAT. But the overall tax savings could far outweigh this.

Download Zone

For a free sample **Deed of Gift**, visit **http://books.indicator.co.uk**. You'll find the access code on page 2 of this book.

What about losses?

If you sell an asset for less than you paid for it, then you have a capital loss. If you make a loss in the same tax year as a capital gain, it's set against the other. If the losses are greater than the gains, then you can carry the excess loss forward and set it against gains in later years. Therefore, you might think that it's a good idea to transfer a loss-making asset to your children so that you can use it to reduce any capital gains you may have.

Trap. Unfortunately, the Taxman thought of this wheeze first. His anti-avoidance rules say that any loss you make on giving an asset to your child can only be used against gains you make on gifts to the same child.

TIP

If there are any unused losses resulting from gifts to a child, these can be carried forward, without a time limit, and used against later gains for the same child.

Solution

Give assets or a share of assets to your children; for CGT purposes these are treated as a sale at market value. When the asset is finally sold to a third party, they will be able to use their annual CGT exemptions to reduce the tax bill on their share of the asset. And you'll be able to use yours against your share.

SECTION 3

Corporation Tax

Getting your hard-earned money out of your company in a tax-efficient way is paramount. But unless you stop the Taxman from eating into your profits, there will be less for you to take out.

This section looks at ways your company can reduce its Corporation Tax liability and how you can avoid some of the most common tax traps.

14.   Buying a brand

Problem

You're thinking of buying a brand from another business to boost your company's sales. But the Taxman is notorious for disallowing a tax deduction for this type of expense.

A brand name and tax

A brand is a so-called "intangible asset". As well as brands this label is also applied to commercial know-how, patents and logos etc., but not research and development expenditure for which there's a different tax treatment.

Broadly, since 2002, a company can obtain Corporation Tax (CT) relief on the amount of depreciation applied in the company's accounts to an intangible asset. The amount you write off against your profit each year is based on generally accepted accounting principles. For example, where your asset has an indefinite life, relief is given at 4% per year on a straight-line basis. And in the year you acquire the asset, the norm is to write a full year's depreciation into those accounts.

Qualifying expenditure

These rules only apply to companies and in respect of intangible assets purchased or created by them after March 31 2002. The tax relief applies to both purchase and development costs.

Example 1

Let's say that in December 2012 you buy the brand of a business at a cost of £50,000. Your company's accounting policy is set to writing this off over five years. Under the **Finance Act 2002**, your company can claim a tax deduction for CT of £10,000 per year. With an effective rate of CT at 20% this will save your company a total of £2,000 a year in tax, i.e. a total of £10,000 over five years.

Where an intangible asset is sold, the profit or loss is treated as a taxable credit or debit rather than as a capital gains transaction.

Example 2

In April 2014 you sell the brand on for £100,000. The cost of £50,000 has already been written off against profits so the whole £100,000 is subject to CT. At a CT rate of, say, 20% this means tax of £20,000.

It's possible to defer any tax on the sale by reinvesting the proceeds into the purchase of new intangible assets. However, you have to reinvest the whole of the proceeds to defer all the tax. The time limit for reinvestment is from one year before until three years after the disposal.

Related parties catch

This tax break doesn't apply where an intangible asset is acquired from a related third party. This would include a close company buying intangible assets from an individual who is a shareholder in that company. For example, no relief is available if you incorporate your own self-employed business and then sell your brand from the old business to your new company in which you have shares. The trap also catches intangible assets sold by one company to another where either company has control of the other. But it doesn't catch transfers between 75% owned group companies where the transferee takes the place of the transferor.

Solution

When purchasing a business comprising intangible assets, you should buy assets rather than shares. The cost of assets such as goodwill can be written off against future profits to obtain CT relief on the purchase price. In contrast, a purchase of shares does not qualify for any relief. However, the seller may have a different view, so be prepared to negotiate with them.

15. Carrying back trading losses

Problem

The temporary rules allowing companies to make more tax-efficient use of trading losses by carrying them back up to three years ended in November 2010. However, in some situations carry-back is still allowed.

Carry-back deadline

At the peak of the credit crunch, the Chancellor announced some extra help for loss-making companies. They would be allowed to carry back trading losses they made in one year to reduce their Corporation Tax (CT) bill in the three previous years. Before this announcement, companies could only carry back losses one year, and if they hadn't paid CT they could only carry forward losses until they had a CT bill to set it against.

Unfortunately the extended carry-back rule came to an end on November 23 2010.

Extended loss carry-back for closing companies

Where you sell or wind up a loss-making business, there's another option that allows you to carry back losses up to three years. This is known as a terminal loss claim. Unlike the temporary tax break, there's no limit on the amount of loss you can carry back.

Download Zone

For a **Terminal Loss Claim**, visit **http://books.indicator.co.uk**. You'll find the access code on page 2 of this book.

Example

Acom Ltd's accounting year runs to December 31. It ceases to trade on November 30 2011. It made profits in 2010 of £12,000 and losses of £88,000 in the eleven months to November 30 2011. The losses in the last twelve months of trading are therefore £87,000, i.e. one month of the 2010 profit being £1,000, and all of the 2011 losses. It can set terminal losses of £87,000 against the CT it has paid on its 2010, 2009 and 2008 profits starting with the latter year first and carrying back any unused losses to the next earliest year.

Trap. Watch out for the Taxman's anti-avoidance rules where you claim terminal losses and then start up a new company carrying on the same trade. The Taxman can retrospectively withdraw the terminal losses in this situation. If you think you might be caught, our advice is to claim the temporary tax break first because the same anti-avoidance rules don't apply.

Solution

Where you're selling or closing down your business and in the final twelve months of trading it makes a loss, don't claim the temporary loss relief tax break mentioned above, opt for a terminal loss claim instead as it's more generous.

16. Different accounting and tax treatment for expenses

Problem

Claiming more expenses reduces your company's tax bill. However, this also reduces the profit figure you might want to show in your accounts to third parties.

Year-end expense problem

Say a company has a financial year-end of March 31 2013. On March 30 it was invoiced for, and paid a fee of, £10,000 for a photo session with an advertising agency. The photo session took place on the same date. The photos will appear in ads during the summer. The company intends to defer showing the expense until its 2014 accounts as it wants to keep the profit in the 2013 accounts as high as possible because it's currently looking for more funding. It justifies this action on the basis that the ads won't generate income until the 2014 financial year. On the other hand, it would like a tax deduction in the 2013 financial year because it incurred the expense in that year.

Treated differently

It's possible for the company to have its cake and eat it by claiming the tax deduction in the earlier year but leaving it out of the accounts until the following year. However, this will usually be the case only where the tax rules differ from the accounting rules. An example would be the capitalisation of interest on a loan to purchase a fixed asset property - the loan relationship rules allow a deduction for the interest when paid, effectively as a tax deduction, despite the fact that it has been treated in the accounts as a capital item. This contrasts with the position where a similar property is purchased and held for development purposes - the capitalised interest will be relieved when the costs are released to the profit and loss account, usually on sale of the property.

Accounting rules

Generally, the tax treatment follows the accounting treatment. Since company accounts should be drawn up under Generally Accepted Accounting Practice (GAAP), the correct treatment in this case is probably, though not necessarily, to include the cost as an expense in the 2013 accounts, and take a tax deduction for the same period.

Taxman's view

As far as HMRC is concerned, the Business Income Manual at **BIM31115** states *"recognise expenditure when incurred unless there is a real and measurable expectation of economic benefit from that expenditure in the future"* (see Appendix).

Timing

In this case, given the timing of the expenditure (one day before the accounting period end) there is a strong argument that the economic benefit flowing from that expenditure would not arise until the following period at the earliest, and so there would be reasonable grounds for prepayment of the majority, if not all, of the expenditure. However, there would be no reasonable grounds for taking an early tax deduction in the 2013 return; a conflict between tax efficiency and commerciality.

Solution

There's no killer solution which will allow you to show a higher profit in your accounts by keeping the expenses figure down while, on the other hand, hiking them up for tax purposes. You should adopt proper accounting treatment for payments in advance (prepayments). This should keep the bank happy, but will involve paying tax earlier.

17. How to manage outside investment

Problem

You've found an individual who's agreed to invest in your company but only on the proviso that the loan you made to your company is waived. This is effectively throwing your money away.

Your loan to the company

You're a director and shareholder of a trading company. Shortly after setting up the company, you put £20,000 of your own money into it which was recorded as a credit balance on your director's loan account. This means it will be included in "other creditors" on the company's balance sheet.

Investor's loan

Your company now needs more funding and you've found someone who's agreed to but only if you waive your loan. This is so that the investor's loan would get priority in the event the company fails and is wound up.

Corporation Tax on waived loans

If you write off your loan, your company will be better off and this credit counts as income and will be taxable. For example, on a £20,000 loan write-off, your company's Corporation Tax bill would go up by £4,000 assuming it pays at the small companies rate (£20,000 x 20%).

Effect on your personal tax

- **Income tax.** Where you write off a loan to your company, you can't claim an income tax deduction for the money you've lost.

- **Capital Gains Tax.** The only situation in which you can claim a Capital Gains Tax loss for the amount of loan you write off is if it has become irrecoverable. Effectively, the company would probably need to be insolvent before a successful claim could be made.

3

Loan priority

This means the investor will know that their loan has priority over the existing loan when it comes to repayment. This alternative means the new lender gets what they want and, since the existing loan isn't written off, no credit needs to be brought into the company's tax computation.

Solution

The company can issue ordinary shares to you in exchange for your loan. You can specify in an agreement that when it comes to distributing the company's assets these shares are lower down the pecking order than the new investor's loan.

18. Loan to an associated company

Problem

There can be good commercial or management reasons for having more than one company. But where these are controlled by the same people it can lead to higher Corporation Tax charges where you shift profits between them.

Separate companies

There are some circumstances in which moving profits from one company to another can be tax efficient. The aim is to shift profit from one to another which has losses or is subject to a lower rate of tax.

Example part 1

Company G, an inactive holding company, has two subsidiaries: H Ltd and I Ltd. The projected profit for the group is £300,000 for the year ended July 31 2012. However, the split of the profits between the two companies is £10,000 from H Ltd and £290,000 from I Ltd. The total CT liability for the group is £67,000 (£2,000 + £65,000). This figure is arrived at as follows:

H Ltd's CT bill on £10,000

PROFITS (£)	CT RATE	CT LIABILITY (£)
On 10,000	20%	2,000
Total		2,000

I Ltd's CT bill on £290,000

PROFITS (£)	CT RATE	CT LIABILITY (£)
On first 150,000	20%	30,000
On next 140,000	25%(*)	35,000
Total £290,000		65,000

(*) Normally the marginal CT rate of 25% doesn't start until profits exceed £300,000. But with two companies it starts at £150,000 (£300,000/2).

In practice you would try to equalise the profit between the companies, for example with the use of a management charge. However, where there are no intercompany services, it might not be possible to justify a management charge. The good news is that there's another solution.

Loan interest - Example part 2

If H limited lends money to I Ltd, it can then charge interest at a commercial rate on the loan. The interest is income in H Ltd's accounts but an expense in I's accounts. In other words, you increase profits taxed at 20% in H Ltd but reduce profits charged at 25% in I Ltd.

Example part 3

If H lends £50,000 to I Ltd at a commercial rate of 9%, the interest figure for twelve months is £4,500; CT saved is £225, i.e. (£4,500 x (25% - 20%)).

TIP

Have a formal loan agreement in place between the two companies to keep the Taxman happy.

Trap. If you charge another company 20% interest in order to shift tax liability, you will have a problem with the Taxman as the rate would not be seen as commercial.

TIP

Before setting an intercompany loan interest rate, check what rate could be achieved by borrowing from the bank. Stay within a point of this and you shouldn't have any trouble.

Solution

Where you want to shift income from one group company to another but there's no ground for charging management fees to achieve this, lend it money on which it has to pay interest.

19. Reducing a group company's tax bill

Problem

You're a shareholder of a company that owns a profitable subsidiary. It shifts its profit to the parent company by paying dividends. But this can result in a higher overall Corporation Tax (CT) bill.

Jumping CT rates

Currently, the main rate of CT is 24% (from April 1 2012) and this applies on all your company's profits if they exceed £300,000. But if they're no more than this, the lower rate of 20% will be charged. So CT is due at 20% on profits of £300,000, but if profits were £300,001 it would be payable at 24% on the lot! But fortunately there's a concession to soften the blow.

Marginal rate relief

Leaping from 20% to 24% tax as a result of making just £1 extra of profit would be unfair, so the Taxman allows you to claim something called marginal rate relief (MRR). This reduces the tax bill by phasing in the higher rate of CT depending on how much profit you make. The higher your profit, the less MRR you can claim. But even with the MRR there's a tax rate trap for companies which own or control one or more others.

Division trap

The amount of profit that can be charged at the lower rate is a maximum of £300,000, so if a company has subsidiaries, it has to share the lower rate band with them.

Example

Where a company has one subsidiary, the £300,000 lower CT band is divided between the two. So they'll both only be allowed up to £150,000 profit chargeable at 20%. This reduced lower rate band means the higher rate of CT kicks in earlier than it does for non-group companies. And if the subsidiary company shifts profit to the parent company by paying a dividend, there's a further problem.

CT MRR problem

In most cases UK dividends received by a company are tax-exempt. That includes those paid by a subsidiary to its parent company. The trouble is that the tax rules say that a dividend doesn't reduce a subsidiary's income for working out the MRR. So in these circumstances a dividend can be very tax inefficient. But there's a possible solution.

TIP

Instead of paying a dividend, the subsidiary could pay its parent company for services it receives from it, e.g. payroll, general admin, accommodation costs, etc. This can be done using a management charge from the parent to the subsidiary. But to avoid running into trouble with the Taxman, the charge must be set at a commercial rate.

Example

XYZ Ltd is a subsidiary in a group of two companies and therefore has a lower CT band of £150,000. In 2012 it had a profit of £180,000, and so it will pay CT at the 2012/13 rate of 24% on this, but it can claim MRR to reduce its overall tax bill. If XYZ pays a dividend to its parent company of £50,000, the CT it must pay is £37,500. But if it pays a management charge of £30,000, its tax bill is cut to £30,000.

Solution

As an alternative to the subsidiary paying the parent company, a dividend can pay a management charge instead. This strategy is only worth using where the subsidiary company's taxable profit exceeds the lower CT rate band and you want to shift income to the parent company.

20. Researching and developing

Problem

Many companies are overlooking the Taxman's special allowance for research and development because, on the face of it, the rules seem complex.

R&D statistics

According to recent statistics, less than 0.5% of companies make a tax claim for research and development (R&D) costs. Based on this it seems many are missing out. And, unlike other tax deductions, you don't just get tax relief on the amount you spend, the Taxman gives you a 125% bonus.

Example

Acom Ltd spends £20,000 on developing a new product. Without R&D relief this expenditure would get Corporation Tax (CT) relief at 20% (assuming it was taxed at the small companies tax rate) meaning that £4,000 would be knocked off its CT bill. However, where the expense qualifies for R&D relief, Acom will get CT relief as if it had spent £4,500. At the 20% CT rate this means a reduction in its tax bill of £9,000.

Trap. For expenditure to qualify for R&D relief it must add up to at least £10,000 in one accounting year. If your R&D expenses won't be much more than this, it's a good idea to timetable the start of an R&D programme at the beginning of your financial year.

What counts as R&D?

A large number of companies are put off claiming R&D because they don't think it applies to them. When you mention "research" it conjures up visions of spectacled boffins crunching numbers or tinkering around with test tubes. But R&D equally applies to technological developments and they don't have to be an obvious feature of an end product. The development can be a technological improvement in a manufacturing process.

TIP

There's no hard and fast rule as to what counts as R&D. And it doesn't matter that the end product isn't a new invention. If making it involves a new technology, it can qualify. For example, if you manufacture machine parts and develop a new technology to improve the process of making them, the money you spend on this counts as R&D.

What expenditure counts?

Where you develop a new system, process, or product which qualifies for R&D relief, some of the costs will be obvious. For example, you might need the input of a designer or other expert and the whole of their fee will qualify. But other expenses can be less obvious, e.g. employee costs.

TIP

You can claim the cost of employees' time, including your own, as an expense for R&D relief. Add together total employment costs, salary, NI, staff welfare etc. and claim the amount which you think was devoted to developing the new product/process. Calculate this as a proportion of the working time employees spent on the project.

Trap. The cost of clerical and administrative work by staff doesn't qualify for R&D relief.

Time limit issues

Since April 2008 the time limit for making R&D claims is two years from the end of the accounting period in which your company incurred the costs.

TIP

Analysing staff and other R&D costs can be a time consuming process. Those experienced in making R&D claims suggest that it saves time and effort by only carrying out the analysis every two years.

Solution

In practice, the R&D rules are more straightforward than they appear. It can be claimed for development of any technological improvement or even a new manufacturing process.

21.　Rolling over a capital gain

Problem

Capital gains made by your company are added to its profits and the total is chargeable to Corporation Tax (CT). Is there a way to defer the tax payable?

Add to profit

Unlike individuals, companies do not pay a separate Capital Gains Tax. Instead, any capital gains are added to the company's income to arrive at the total amount chargeable to CT.

For example, say your company sells its existing premises at a profit. The calculations are quite straightforward; proceeds of the sale are £300,000, less costs of £120,000, this leaves a taxable gain of £180,000. Assuming the gain plus its taxable trading profits for the year don't exceed £300,000, your company would pay CT on this at 20%. So the CT bill is £36,000.

Rollover relief

A capital gain from a (qualifying) asset can be "rolled over" against the purchase of another (qualifying) asset by the same company (or another company in a group of companies). This rollover relief is deducted from the cost of the new asset(s), which means that when it's eventually sold the original capital gain will be taxed as part of the gain on the new asset.

Where your company uses the sale proceeds to help fund the purchase of a bigger and better property, say, two adjacent units on a business park, then the gain can be deducted from the cost of the two units. So there is no immediate CT bill for your company.

Telling the Taxman

When your company submits its accounts and CT return for the accounting year in which the property was sold, it will make a rollover claim at the same time.

TIP

Delay finalising your rollover claim for as long as possible; once submitted (and accepted by the Taxman) it can't be revised. If your business is rolling over a gain into two or more assets, submit a provisional claim. In other words, claim provisional rollover relief based on assumed facts. You don't need to finalise the claim for another four years - and who knows what might happen in that time.

Download Zone

For a **Sample Rollover Claim**, visit **http://books.indicator.co.uk**. You'll find the access code on page 2 of this book.

TIP

When you do eventually submit the full claim, you choose how to match the acquisition(s) against the disposal(s). You may be able to save a great deal of tax by matching most or all of the original sale proceeds against asset(s) which you don't intend to sell.

Solution

You can defer paying tax on a capital gain by reinvesting in new business assets. As long as a rollover relief claim is in force, your company will not be required to pay tax on the original sale. However, the key thing with any rollover claim is to take your time. It costs you nothing to keep your options open with a provisional claim.

22. Reducing the tax cost of selling a company

Problem

Where your company sells its investment in another, the Taxman will often treat any profit made on the deal as tax-exempt. But where the exemption doesn't apply, any gain made will be subject to Corporation Tax.

What counts as an exempt gain?

In 2002 the Taxman introduced a tax break for companies called the Substantial Shareholdings Exemption (SSE). The effect of this is to exempt from Corporation Tax any capital gain (profit) made by your company from selling shares it owns in other companies.

The main conditions of the exemption are that your company must own at least 10% of the other company's shares. So where you get an offer you can't refuse to sell a subsidiary, i.e. a company in which you own over 50% of the ordinary shares, you would expect any gain made to be tax-free.

If your company or the subsidiary isn't a trading company, e.g. they are inactive or exist to mainly manage investments, the SSE won't apply, and the gain will be taxable. But there is a way to reduce the gain.

Reducing the gain

An alternative solution to the SSE would be to ask for less money for the company; less money equals less gain, and less gain equals less tax. This doesn't sound too attractive an idea so far, but there's a little more to this scheme.

If, over the years, the subsidiary company has accumulated profits, these are known as "distributable reserves"; it can pay these out as dividends to the shareholder, i.e. your company, before the sale. Obviously, as the subsidiary has paid out its reserves it won't be worth as much as before; therefore, the amount the buyer will pay for the shares will be less.

Example

Acom Ltd owns all the shares in a property rental company. It's offered £510,000 for it. The subsidiary has built up reserves of £300,000 which it pays as a dividend to Acom. As a result, the buyer reduces their offer by £300,000. Overall, Acom gets the same amount out of the deal.

	ORIGINAL OFFER FOR SHARES	PRE-SALE DIVIDEND	OFFER AFTER DIVIDEND
Sales proceeds	£510,000	£300,000	£210,000
Less cost of shares, say	£10,000		£10,000
Gain liable to CT	£500,000		£200,000
CT payable at 20%	£100,000		£40,000
CT saving			£60,000

Acom reduced the sale proceeds of its subsidiary by £300,000 and received a dividend instead. In doing so it saved £60,000 in CT. And here's the punch line: dividends received by companies are exempt from CT, so Acom doesn't have to pay a penny tax on the £300,000.

Trap. There are anti-avoidance rules to stop companies from artificially inflating the value of their reserves so they pay out higher pre-sale dividends to increase the tax saving. (See Appendix for a weblink to what the Taxman has to say about applying the rules.)

Solution

Where the gain you make from selling shares in another company won't be covered by the Substantial Shareholdings Exemption, ask the company to make a pre-sale dividend to clear out its built up profits. You can then afford to sell the shares for less and so reduce your CT bill.

23. Tax deduction for unpaid interest

Problem

To ease cash flow you're leaving the dividends due to you in the company, but you want it to pay you interest for having the use of your money. The trouble is it can't afford to pay that either, but can it still claim the tax relief for it?

Charging your company interest

A profit shown in your accounts doesn't necessarily mean cash in the bank. So although a company can vote dividends, it may not be able to afford to pay them. Instead, you could allow them to accumulate in your director's loan account. In this situation there's nothing to stop you charging your company interest on the amount it owes you.

Example - part 1

Ron owns 50% of the shares in Acom Ltd. Over the years he has ploughed back his dividends to provide working capital. In Acom's financial year ended December 31 2012 the credit on Ron's loan account was £100,000 throughout. Ron charged Acom interest at 5% per annum on the loan. The interest due to him is £5,000 but Acom doesn't pay it. If it claims the interest in its 2012 accounts, it would reduce its Corporation Tax (CT) bill by £1,000 (£5,000 x 20%).

Unpaid interest

The Taxman's "loan relationship" rules dictate the amount of interest on which your company can claim CT relief. They say that in most situations tax relief can be claimed on interest due, even when it hasn't yet been paid.

Trap. A loan to a close company, i.e. one that's controlled by five or fewer people, made by a shareholder is subject to the anti-avoidance "late interest rule". This means a company can't claim a CT deduction unless it pays the interest within twelve months after the end of its financial year. If it doesn't, it has to wait for a tax deduction in the year in which it actually pays the interest.

Example - part 2

Following on from our example above, Acom can claim CT relief for the year ended December 31 2012 provided the interest is paid to Ron by December 31 2012. However, to count as paid, the interest can't simply be added as a credit to Ron's loan account, he must actually receive it.

If Acom defers paying the interest to the last minute, i.e. until December 31 2012, it will still be allowed the CT relief claimed in its December 31 2012 profits.

Shareholder's tax deferral

By deferring the payment of interest to Ron until after the start of the next tax year, April 6 2012, it won't count as his income for self-assessment (SA) purposes until 2012/13. And under SA, Ron won't have to pay tax on the interest until January 31 2014.

Double your money

Ron could easily justify a 10% interest rate, rather than the 5% he charged on his unsecured high-risk loan to Acom. This would double the amount of interest due to him to £10,000. He could then afford to sacrifice salary equal to the extra interest he has received, i.e. £5,000. This would save both him and Acom money as there's no NI payable on interest. On £5,000 of interest paid instead of earnings this would save up to around £1,200.

TIP

Always charge the maximum rate of interest you think can commercially be justified on money you loan your company. Sacrifice some of your salary to compensate for the extra money you're taking as interest. This will reduce both your NI bills.

Solution

The company can delay the interest payment to you for up to twelve months and still claim a tax deduction for it in the year the interest was due. You only have to pay tax on the interest for the year in which you receive it.

24. Overdrawn loan accounts and dividends

Problem

It comes to light during the preparation of your company's accounts that you have an overdrawn director's loan account. Should you take a dividend from the company and repay it or just leave the amount owing to the company?

Director's loan account

When checking your March 31 2012 accounts in order to prepare the 2011/12 tax return, your accountant notices that your director's account was overdrawn by just under £1,000. If the loan account is not returned to credit within nine months of your company's year-end, the tax rules say that your company has to pay tax equal to 25% of the amount which remains overdrawn. This tax will be refunded on the due date for the payment of the CT bill for the period in which the loan was fully repaid.

This is a significant period of time to be deprived of funds. The tax charge and the loss of funds continue all the while the matter is not addressed. So the price of inaction can become relatively expensive.

Even if in the past you have left earnings in the company taking no salary or dividends, be aware of the overdrawn loan account trap when you next decide to take a dividend, as this can provide a solution.

Example

Assuming your loan account is overdrawn by £1,000, you could take a dividend to clear this. Consequently, you are only comparing the tax on a dividend with the 25% tax payable by your company for making a loan to you. If the shareholder (you) is a higher rate taxpayer (40%), the effective rate of tax is 22.5%. A dividend of £1,000 is grossed to take account of a one-ninth tax credit. The taxable dividend plus tax credit is therefore £1,111 (£1,000 x ten ninths). This is taxed at 32.5% (£361). But you then deduct the tax credit of £111 from this to arrive at the your personal self-assessment tax bill for the dividend, i.e. £250. The tax the company has to pay if the loan account isn't cleared is also £250.

Therefore, if you're comparing tax on a dividend with tax on a loan, there is no difference apart from timing. The loan will need to be repaid at some point and so, in normal circumstances, the question is whether to pay a dividend to be taxed through self-assessment, payable on January 31 after the year-end, or let the company pay an equal amount of tax, but knowing that this will be refunded after the overdrawn loan account has been repaid.

Solution

Draw an extra dividend and then use this to clear your loan account. If your loan account is not returned to credit within nine months of your company's year-end, the Taxman imposes a 25% tax charge. In terms of cash flow, payment of personal tax on an additional dividend is better than repaying 100% of the loan account from private funds.

SECTION 4

Expenses and benefits

Not all pay is in the form of wages or salary; most companies offer their directors and staff some perks or expenses. The Taxman has a special set of rules for valuing these; it's his so-called "benefits code".

The benefits code contains some of the most complex rules in the tax system, but complexity always leads to loopholes. This section tells you how you can use them to your advantage.

25. Advance expenses tax efficiently

Problem

You have already borrowed £5,000, the maximum tax-free loan, from your company. But you need a further advance to cover business expenses; will this mean a tax bill?

What counts as a loan?

A loan means more than just lending money, in fact according to the Taxman, it includes *"any kind of advance by reason of employment is a loan"*. For example, any amount shown in the employer's books or records as owed to the company by a director or employee will count as a loan - **HMRC Booklet 490 Expense and Benefits A Tax Guide** (see Appendix for a weblink).

Loan exemption

As long as the total you owe the company at any time doesn't exceed £5,000 during the tax year, the loan(s) won't count as a taxable benefit-in-kind. This limit is referred to as the "normal £5,000 threshold" in s.180 of the **Income Tax (Employment and Pensions) Act 2003 (ITEPA)**.

This is an all or nothing exemption. If, however briefly, the loan balance rises above £5,000 in the tax year, the exemption is not available. Where an employee with a loan of £5,000 borrows another £1,000, even for just a few days, he or she will have a tax liability because the total loan balance of £6,000 exceeded the £5,000 tax-free exemption. Employers' NI will also be due on what is now a taxable benefit-in-kind.

Record keeping

It's important to keep a running total of amounts borrowed if you intend to keep within the £5,000 tax-free limit. You'll also need this information where the limit is exceeded and you need to work out the benefit-in-kind to declare on the annual benefits and expenses return Form P11D.

Loan advance for expenses

An advance to cover future business expenses is a loan for tax purposes. However, s.179 of ITEPA overrides the benefit-in-kind rules.

The conditions that need to be satisfied are:

- the maximum amount advanced at any one time must not exceed £1,000
- advances must be spent within six months; and
- the employee must regularly account to their employer for how they spent the amount advanced.

TIP

S.179 of ITEPA also contains a clause which says that where you need to advance expenses of more than £1,000, say for a foreign business trip, you can write to the Taxman and ask him to increase the limit.

Solution

You can use the special exemption in s.179 of ITEPA to make tax-free advance expenses of up to £1,000. This won't affect the £5,000 tax-free loan rule. And if you want to advance more than £1,000, you can write to the Taxman and ask for the limit to be increased.

26. Mileage allowances for contractors

Problem

You want to cut the costs involved when paying contractors, but obviously they aren't too keen. How can you achieve your target and keep them happy by paying mileage allowance payments?

Who can use the Approved Mileage Allowance Payments Scheme?

Where you pay your employees for business journeys made in their own car or van, you can use the Taxman's approved rate - AMAPS. (See Appendix for the current AMAPS rates.) These payments are tax and NI-free. But by concession the Taxman allows self-employed workers to claim the same amount tax deductible whether or not they actually incur that amount of expense. You can use this concession to your advantage when paying self-employed contractors.

Trap. Only self-employed workers whose gross earnings are less than the VAT registration limit, currently £70,000 per year, can use this concession.

Offering a tax-free travel allowance

You can suggest to your contractors that you'll pay them an allowance for their travel that you can guarantee will be tax-free. This will take the place of an equal amount of the money they charge you for their work. This can give them a tax advantage.

Example

Bob is a kitchen fitter and you put a great deal of work his way. On average he drives about 14,000 miles for you each year. He's just bought a small two-year-old diesel van for £4,500. He uses it for private journeys 20% of the time. He reckons he'll keep the van three years and then sell it. His tax position might be as follows:

If Bob's general van costs are £2,300 each year (see calculation below), he can claim the business use proportion, that's 80%, i.e. £1,840, and all the fuel costs for business trips, which are £1,550. So he'll get tax relief on £3,390 in total. But if he claims the Taxman's AMAPS rate instead, he'll get tax relief on £5,500 (10,000 miles at 45p and 4,000 miles at 25p). By doing this he'll get tax relief on an extra £1,610 each year. Over three years that's £4,830. That will save Bob £1,352 in tax and Class 4 NI. That's good for him, but you came up with the idea so why shouldn't you gain? (For the full calculation in this example see the Appendix.)

Working out the savings

Obviously, you would need to work out the numbers with your own contractors; you can use our workings as a guide. If the result is a healthy profit, we suggest that you split the tax saving 50:50. This can be done by the contractor reducing their bill.

TIP 1

Substitute some of what you would pay a contractor for a tax-free mileage allowance and agree a discount on their bill to get a share of the tax they'll save.

TIP 2

Although it's up to the contractor to keep a mileage log for their accounting records and for the Taxman, we recommend that you do it too. You'll know where you've sent the contractor for each job, so it shouldn't be difficult to work out the mileage and calculate the amount you need to pay them against their invoice.

Solution

Pay your contractors AMAPS for their work travel in place of some of their normal fees. This will be tax and NI-free for them, so use this saving to renegotiate what you pay them.

27.   Alternative to the office party

Problem

You normally have an annual party for your employees which the Taxman accepts as a tax-free benefit for directors and employees alike. But the format is getting a little tired; what can you offer as a tax-free alternative?

Party exemption

Where your company throws a party for all its employees and the cost will not count as a taxable benefit-in-kind where its less than £150 per head (s.264 of the **Income Tax Earnings and Pensions Act 2003** (ITEPA)). But you were thinking of changing the arrangement this year by giving your employees a voucher for a meal at a local restaurant and keeping the cost within £150.

Most vouchers are liable to tax and must be reported on Form P11D. NI is also payable through the payroll in the month the voucher is gifted.

Trap. The tax rules contain an exemption for vouchers which *"can only be used to obtain anything the direct provision of which would fall within s.264"* and it's quite clear from s.266(3) of ITEPA that the exemption extends to a voucher that's exchangeable for an annual staff party or similar function, i.e. a ticket to go to the party. But taking your employees out, or allowing them to go for a meal singly, or in small groups, is not within the £150 exemption. The whole point of a staff party is that it has to be collective.

Party bag alternative

To spice up the annual bash you can include a gift as part of the celebrations. For example, a hamper at the Christmas do. As long as the total cost of the function including the gift is less than the £150 per head limit it will be a tax and NI-free benefit.

Panto or day at the races

The £150 exemption can also apply to a trip out for your employees as long as everyone is invited. For example, a day at the races or the theatre, perhaps to see the Panto.

Solution

As an alternative to the usual annual party you can take your employees to the theatre, for example. As long as the cost per head stays within the £150 limit it will be tax and NI-free for them. If this isn't a popular idea you could just perk up the party by including a gift for everyone, e.g. a hamper. Again, as long as the cost of the gift and the party together are no more than £150, then it's all tax and NI-free.

28. Income Protection Insurance

Problem

You're considering introducing Income Protection Insurance as a staff benefit. But for tax purposes there are two different ways of doing this; each has tax advantages and disadvantages, but you want the best of both.

Exempt benefits

Permanent Health Insurance (PHI), also known as Income Protection Insurance (IPI), can be taken out by individuals. It will provide them with income if they're unable to work as a result of ill-health or disability, or even redundancy. Where a claim is made on the policy, any amount paid out is tax-free by virtue of a special exemption, s.735 of the **Income Tax (Trading and Other Income) Act 2005** (ITTOIA). But where an employer takes out a group scheme and pays the premium as a benefit-in-kind (BiK) there are tax consequences.

Group scheme tax rules

The Taxman's guidance on PHI/IPI is not very clear. But we can say for certain that the exemption mentioned above is extended to employees who benefit from a policy taken out on their behalf by their employer (s.743 ITTOIA 2005). But there's a catch when the policy pays out.

The Taxman's instruction manual at **IPTM6120** says *"...if it [the premium] were taxed as a benefit the employee would have, in effect, paid the premium out of taxed income. Payments received under the policy would therefore be exempt."*

Trap. The tax-free status on PHI/IPI payouts is lost where the insured, i.e. the employee, doesn't have to pay tax as a BiK on the premiums paid by their employer. This means they will have to pay tax on money they receive as a payout from the policy.

Paying tax on the premium instead

Where an employer pays a PHI/IPI premium for an employee who is charged to tax on this as a BiK, there will be no tax to pay on the income received if and when the policy pays out.

Tax on premium or tax on payout - which is better?

It seems that one way or the other the Taxman is going to get his pound of flesh. But we think there's a neat solution to reduce the tax payable.

TIP

PHI/IPI policy premiums are due in advance, which means that you can use hindsight to decide whether to declare PHI/IPI premiums for employees under a group scheme as a taxable BiK. That way you can choose the most tax-efficient option.

Example

Assume on May 1 2012 you pay the premium renewal for all your employees included under a group PHI/IPI scheme. It averages out at £1,500 per employee. If no one claims under the policy by the end of the tax year, you can ignore the premium when the time comes to declare BiKs on Form P11D in July 2013. Therefore, no employee has to pay tax on the premium. But now assume that one of your employees falls ill in November 2012 and can't work. They claim £7,500 on the policy up to the end of the tax year. When it comes to filling in their P11D you can include the premium, just for that employee, as a BiK. They won't be taxed on the £7,500 but only on the £1,500 premium. Tax is avoided on £6,000!

(See Appendix for a weblink to the Taxman's view of PHI/IPI on his website.)

Solution

Declaring premiums as a taxable BiK on Form P11D will mean that any policy payouts are tax-free, and vice versa. But because you don't have to decide which of these tax treatments applies until after the end of each tax year, by which time you'll know whether a claim has been made, you can choose to tax the premium or the payout, depending on which costs you the least amount of tax.

29. Personal use of company assets

Problem

The company is considering purchasing a helicopter to fly the directors to business meetings. But if it's also used privately will there be tax to pay, and how can you keep this to a minimum?

Who's taxable?

The tax rules say that an employee or director can be liable to tax where a company asset is *made available* to them for private use, even where they don't actually use it.

Example

A company with three directors purchased a helicopter for £105,000. Only one director has a licence to fly it. The helicopter will be used for business journeys, a log of which will be kept.

While some assets, e.g. cars, have special rules for working out the taxable benefit-in-kind, the tax bill for private use of a helicopter is based on its "annual value" plus the additional expenses incurred in providing the asset (s.205 of the **Income Tax (Earnings and Pensions) Act 2003** (ITEPA)).

What's the annual value?

The annual value of an asset is 20% its market value at the time it was first available for private use. But if the helicopter were rented or hired, rather than owned outright, the rental cost would be used instead if it were greater. Therefore, if the helicopter was bought for £105,000, each director to which it was available will be charged 20% of this, i.e. £21,000, as a benefit-in-kind (BiK). Tax at 40% on £21,000 is £8,400 for having the chance to fly/ride in the helicopter for private journeys.

Additional expenses will include running costs and may include expenditure on alterations or improvements, repairs, maintenance etc. depending on whether it was incurred for the purpose of providing the benefit (see Appendix for a weblink to HMRC Employment Income Manual at para **EIM21631**). In the case of the helicopter, it will certainly include fuel, insurance and repairs.

4

Business use reduction

Under s.365 of ITEPA 2003, where there's both business and private use, the director is entitled to a reduction in the BiK for the proportion that is for business use.

Tip 1

In practice, you can agree with the Taxman that the log of journeys and flying hours provides a convenient measure of the helicopter's use. Take a copy of this and annotate each flight as business or private according to its primary purpose. The number of business hours as a proportion to total hours flown for the year can then be used as the basis of a claim to reduce the cash equivalent (both the annual value and the additional expenditure).

Tip 2

Apply for, and obtain, a PAYE dispensation from reporting the full amount on Form P11D. This is also the opportunity to agree the method of calculating the benefit.

Download Zone

For a **PAYE Dispensation Application**, visit **http://books.indicator.co.uk**. You'll find the access code on page 2 of this book.

Trap. The bad news is that for NI there's no equivalent to the income tax rule, which taxes only a proportion of the cost where there is mixed business and private use. Therefore, the employer's NI charge arises on the full amount of the benefit.

Benefit spreading

The rules say that where the asset isn't available for the whole tax year, or where there's more than one director using it, the BiK could be apportioned between the directors (see Appendix for a weblink to the Taxman's manuals at para **EIM21200**). The helicopter's log showing the passengers carried on private trips should be a suitable basis of apportionment.

Solution

To minimise the tax charge on the private use of a company helicopter, keep a copy of the flight log which clearly shows the purpose of each trip. You can spread the charge between the number of directors/employees who can use it and reduce the resulting tax bill by the proportion of business use.

SECTION 5

Inheritance Tax

Once just a problem for the rich, Inheritance Tax is now hitting many families with more modest wealth. This has meant Inheritance Tax has enjoyed a great deal of publicity in the last few years; transferable nil rate bands and high property values being just two of the hot topics.

This section shows some of the steps you can take to shift income out of your estate in a tax-effective way; in some cases while maintaining an income from the wealth you've given away.

30. Giving away property

Problem

You plan to save Inheritance Tax (IHT) by giving your holiday home to your children, yet retain the right to use it sometimes. But if you do the Taxman will still treat it as yours.

Continued use of a gift

As part of your financial planning you gave your holiday home to your children; it was worth £200,000 at the time, so your estate could save IHT of up to £80,000. All you now have to do is survive for seven years and the property is no longer part of your estate. But you still want to use the property for a few weeks a year.

Reserved benefit

The Taxman's rule is that if you make a gift but continue to have use of the asset, then in his eyes you have "reserved a benefit" and not really given it away at all. The Taxman has a point and he can be very strict on what constitutes a benefit.

For example, if you made a gift, of say, some antique chairs, to your son and used them when you visited him, the Taxman might argue that you are deriving a benefit and treat them as still yours for IHT purposes.

The law

S.102(1)(b) of the **Finance Act 1986** says that if you make a gift, it will remain part of your estate for IHT purposes unless you are "virtually entirely" excluded from using or benefiting from it. So how much is "virtually entirely"? If your view differs from the Taxman's, your beneficiaries will have an uphill battle to avoid IHT.

> ### Tip
>
> You could pay the market rate for the use of the property. The Taxman will then accept there is no reservation of benefit.

Trap. Rent for use of the holiday home could run into thousands of pounds each year. Unfortunately, that's not the end of the story; it gets worse.

Income tax consequence

Paying rent may save you from the Taxman's IHT trap but now your children may have to pay income tax on the rent they receive from you. They will also have to manage the corresponding record keeping for their tax returns.

Solution

Only give your children a share of the property and retain a share for yourself. The share you give away will, subject to the seven-year rule mentioned above, not be part of your estate for IHT purposes.

As long as you all have use of the property and equally share the running costs, the Taxman will accept that there is no reservation of benefit and so not be part of your estate for IHT. Once you have transferred the property into joint names you need to make sure expenses are shared.

Set up a joint bank account with your children solely for handling the property-related transactions. Each pay in an equal amount. The running costs can now be paid from this account ensuring that they are equally shared.

31. A DIY IHT loan plan

Problem

It's standard IHT planning to make gifts of your assets of up to £3,000 per year to use your IHT annual exemption. But this will only chip away at the potentially massive IHT bill on your estate.

Give it away

The key to avoiding IHT is giving away your wealth at the earliest possible opportunity. Of course, we don't mean you should hand money over to anyone for the sake of it, although that would work, you'll want to pass it on to your children, grandchildren, nieces, nephews etc. But if you die within seven years of making the gift, the Taxman will treat the money as part of your estate and charge IHT accordingly.

Gifts ignored for IHT

The Taxman ignores gifts you make of up to £3,000 per year. There are a few other exemptions, however these are aimed at specific types of gift, e.g. to those getting married, and they don't add up to much. Plus, while you might be happy to make gifts of a few thousand pounds a year, you're not comfortable handing over tens of thousands. It's the classic IHT dilemma: to get the capital out of your estate you have to give it away, but if you do that it won't be there in the event of an emergency. And worse still, at least from a tax point of view, is that it's growing in value all the time and so increasing the potential IHT bill.

IHT freezing

The insurance industry offers a couple of IHT avoidance solutions in the form of discounted gift and loan schemes. Both these do the job of getting money out of your estate and, at the same time, can generate an income for you. But they have drawbacks.

Trap. Like all insurance products they cost money. The insurance company and your financial advisor won't be setting the scheme up as a freebie. A further drawback is that they tend to be inflexible. Once you've handed your money over, you're committed to the terms of the scheme.

Interest-free loan

As an alternative to insurance products or making a straight gift to the intended beneficiary, give them an interest-free, open-ended loan, which they can then use to buy investments. The income the investment money generates will be part of their estate for IHT purposes and not yours.

Example

Bob makes a loan of £100,000 to his son John which he invests in a combination of shares and cash deposits. Over the following ten years these produce £30,000 of income and £20,000 in capital growth. This all belongs to John. Had it been in Bob's name the £50,000 increase in value would have been part of his estate and so could have resulted in an IHT bill of £20,000 (£50,000 x 40%).

Solution

A loan can be a convenient way to use your IHT annual exemption. All you need do is write off up to £3,000 of the loan each year. This counts as a gift because it reduces the amount of money you'll get back.

Draw up an agreement that gives you the right to ask for the balance of the loan to be repaid at any time (see the Appendix for recommended terms and conditions to include in a loan).

32. Loan and discounted gift schemes

Problem

The mantra of the Inheritance Tax (IHT) planner is *"give away as much as you can, as soon as you can"*. But what if you can't afford to give away your assets just to save IHT because you need the income they produce. How can you reduce a potential IHT bill and keep your income?

Insurance

Certain insurance-based schemes allow you to retain some income from your investments whilst reducing the value of your estate for IHT purposes. There are two similar plans that allow for a regular predictable income; these are known as "loan schemes" and "discounted gift schemes".

Discounted gift schemes

These plans offer IHT savings to people who, whilst wanting income from their assets, can afford to give away the capital outright. The schemes require you to invest a lump sum which will be invested into a bond in return for an annuity paid to you. Commonly, this will be at the rate of 5% per annum and is tax-free.

Some schemes pay higher annuity rates but these rely on an assessment of your health and life expectancy. A small part of these annuity payments would be taxable. We recommend that if you want to find out how much you could receive as income, you should obtain quotes from more than one insurance company. Most of the well known insurers offer these types of schemes so it shouldn't be hard to do.

The bond you purchase is placed into a trust for the beneficiaries of your estate. The annuity you receive is set at an amount so that its long-term value is less than the value of the bond. The difference between these values is "discounted", i.e. it immediately falls out of your estate for IHT purposes rather than having to wait seven years as is usual for gifts.

Loan schemes

This type of scheme allows the investor to draw on capital rather than income, but as a consequence is not as efficient at saving IHT. The intention of the scheme is to stop the growth in your estate from being chargeable to IHT.

Example

If you made an investment of £100,000 into a loan scheme, the increase in value of that investment, usually over 20 years, could be significant but it won't be part of your estate for IHT purposes.

The plan requires that you make a loan into a trust which is repaid to you, usually interest-free, over a 20-year term, thus giving you a regular income. The trust uses the loan to purchase an investment bond of the type that allows withdrawals of 5% tax-free per annum, which therefore provides enough money to repay the loan to you.

TIP

Using a discounted gift scheme you can reduce the value of your estate for IHT purposes immediately. With a loan scheme you can reduce the value of your estate over time.

Solution

Purchase a discount gift scheme from an insurance company. The insurance linked schemes include an element of gift to the beneficiaries named in the policy, which will therefore reduce your estate for IHT. But it will also pay you an income. Where you need access to the capital, you could use a loan scheme instead.

SECTION 6

Miscellaneous

Tax is a fact of life whether you're an individual paying through self-assessment or a company paying Corporation Tax. Tax breaks are equally diverse.

In this section there are tax-saving tips for everyone from business entrepreneurs to property investors and others.

33.   A trust for school fees

Problem

One of the problems with paying school fees or any of the costs of bringing up children is that it all comes out of your taxed income. How can you get around this?

Unused tax allowances

All individuals, including children, are entitled to claim a personal allowance which they can use to reduce the amount of income on which they pay tax. For individuals under 65 the annual amount is currently £8,105 (for 2012/13). In most cases children don't have sufficient income to use up their personal allowance.

Investment income

If the children had income-generating investments in their own name, these tax-free allowances would not be wasted. So with some simple planning you can make investments in your child's name which generate income to meet future school fees, but which also utilise these tax-free allowances.

Trap. If a parent provides their child with an investment, the Taxman will tax the income (if it exceeds £100) as if it belongs to the parent, so there is no tax saving.

Tip

However, if a grandparent (or other relative) provides an invest-ment, the income will belong to the child for tax purposes.

Rental income scheme - using a trust

Another way to give a child an income and use up their personal allowances is for their grandparent (or any relative except their parents) to transfer enough capital to them for a rental property to be purchased. Of course they wouldn't want your children to have control over the property, so it could be held in a trust with you as a trustee. Normally, this would be done under an accumulation and maintenance (A&M) type of trust, which your solicitor can easily prepare an appropriate trust deed for.

School fees

In our scenario, the trust's bank account is used to deposit the rental income and then pay out school fees at the discretion of the trustees. None of the A&M trust's beneficiaries has an automatic right to either income or capital, although it must have been handed over by the time one of the beneficiaries reaches the age of 18 or there can be an Inheritance Tax (IHT) charge where the value of the gift exceeds the IHT nil rate band, see below.

Funding the trust - a warning

Unless the grandparents put, for example, a property into the A&M trust soon after they've acquired it, there is a potential Capital Gains Tax problem for them.

Tax repayments

Once the property is in the trust, the trustees can use the rents to pay school fees. Trustees are required to deduct income tax at 50% from the payments, so they should pay 50% in school fees and 50% to the Taxman. You can then reclaim the 50% tax on your children's income up to £8,105 each (that's a repayment of £3,738 being £7,475 x 50%). Recycle this to pay further school fees each year.

Warning. New trusts will suffer an IHT charge on each ten-year anniversary of the original settlement date, and exit charges if the assets pass out of the trust. However, if the value of the trust is less than the nil rate band, currently £325,000, then there will be no IHT to pay.

Solution

With a rental property in an A&M type of trust for your children, 60% of the rents can be used to pay their school fees. Although the other 40% goes to the Taxman, claim tax back by using the children's own tax-free allowances.

34. Making a profit from Gift Aid

Problem

It's nice to do your bit for charity by making a donation. It's even better when the Taxman rewards you by knocking a bit off your tax bill for your generosity. But how can you make a profit on the deal?

Tax relief on donations

When you donate some cash to a charity these days you're usually prompted to tick the box on the donation slip or envelope that says something like *"I am a UK taxpayer and want to make this gift under the Gift Aid arrangements"*. This allows your chosen charity to get a boost in the form of a tax credit of 25p for every pound you give them. So when you donate £1 they'll actually receive £1.25 in their coffers. There's nothing new about that, but for higher rate taxpayers there's an added incentive.

New incentive to give

If you pay tax at the higher rate, your £1 will not only earn the charity an extra 25p from the Taxman but you'll get a similar tax break. So, for example, if you make a donation under Gift Aid of £200 to your local church, the Taxman will gross this up to £250. The church (providing it's a registered charity) can claim back the extra £50 and you can claim back higher rate tax on the gross donation, i.e. £250 x (40% higher rate tax - 20% basic rate tax) = £50.

Additional tax rate

The additional tax rate of 50% introduced with effect from April 6 2010 is not actually the highest rate of income tax you can pay. The top rate of 50% only applies to those whose taxable income exceeds £150,000. In practice, those with taxable incomes between £100,000 and £116,210 face tax at 60%. This is because you'll lose one pound of your tax-free allowances for every pound of taxable income you have over £100,000. As the basic tax allowances for 2012/13 are £8,105, when your income reaches £116,210 your basic-tax-free allowance will have been reduced to zero.

6

Miscellaneous

Extra tax relief

If you're unlucky enough to fall into the 60% tax bracket, there's one bit of good news. Your Gift Aid donation to charity of, say, £200 will cost you just £100 net compared to £150 net in 2009/10.

> **TIP**
>
> Get some payback from the increased tax rates. Some organisations, such as the National Trust, have gift aid membership arrangements. So, if in 2012/13 a family membership costs, say, £105, the cost to you after tax relief at the maximum 2012/13 rate of 60% will be just £63.

Increase giving to save tax

Most people are aware of the tax relief they can get for charitable cash donations, but not many realise that if you make a gift, say, to a charity shop, that can be converted by them into a cash donation on which tax relief is available.

Example

Bob has ripped a copy of his complete CD collection onto his PC and so decides to free some space at home by donating the 300 discs to a charity shop. They log all these in Bob's name and as they sell them the proceeds are treated as a cash donation. Let's say they get £900 for the CDs. This is treated as a cash donation by Bob and is grossed up by the Taxman to £1,125. The charity receives the extra £225 and Bob can claim higher rate tax relief on the gross donation. That could be up to a £450 tax refund for him. (For more information on tax rates and details of charities who operate the Gift Aid for goods scheme see the Appendix.)

Solution

There's now greater tax relief than ever on Gift Aid payments. A £250 donation could cost you just £100 net. Make donations of items to a charity shop for them to sell. This will cost you nothing but still qualify for Gift Aid relief, which means you'll make a profit on the deal. For example, if a charity shop got £900 for your old CD collection, you could receive up to £450 back from the Taxman.

35. EIS carry-back restrictions scrapped

Problem

The Enterprise Investment Scheme rules changed in 2009 allowing more flexibility over when you can claim income tax relief for making this type of investment. But you need to watch the rules carefully if you want to maximise this.

Incentive

If you're not familiar with Enterprise Investment Schemes (EISs), the idea behind them is to give tax breaks to investors in small to medium sized companies. That can be high risk, but investment banks etc. have developed schemes to spread your EIS investment over a number of companies and so reduce the chance of losing money. The tax breaks take two forms: Capital Gains Tax and income tax (see the Appendix).

EIS - old rules

The income tax relief EIS investors can claim is always at the same rate. It doesn't matter whether you pay tax at the higher or the basic rate, you can claim a credit against your income tax bill equal to 20% of your investment. As a small but additional perk the Taxman allowed you to carry back up to half of the tax relief against your tax bill for the previous year. This allowed you to get your hands on the tax relief sooner.

Example - old rules

In September 2008 Louise invested £30,000 in an EIS fund. She received confirmation (Certificate EIS5) from the fund managers in March 2009 that the conditions had been met for her to claim tax relief. She sent the certificate to her tax office and asked the Taxman to carry back the tax relief to the 2007/8 tax year and the rest to be allowed for 2008/9. The Taxman credited her self-assessment account as follows:

TAX YEAR	CALCULATION	TAX RELIEF GIVEN
2007/8	£15,000 x 20%	£3,000
2008/9	£15,000 x 20%	£3,000

Note. The EIS maximum investment allowed is £500,000 per annum. But the maximum tax relief that could be carried back was only 50% of the investment, or £50,000, whichever was lower. And you couldn't carry back any relief at all if your investment was made between October 6 and the following April 5.

Improved carry-back rule

The **Finance Act 2009** abolished the restrictions that applied to the carry back of income tax relief. An investment in an EIS after April 21 2009 can be carried back in full the previous year. That could have a far more significant effect on your self-assessment tax payments than you might think.

Tip

Making an EIS investment by April 5 2013 could reduce your self-assessment payments by an amount equal to 40% of the amount invested.

Example

Louise recently submitted her self-assessment tax form showing her 2011/12 tax bill as £16,000. The self-assessment rules set her payments on account (POA) for 2012/13 at the same level. She made one POA of £8,000 on January 31 2011 and with another £8,000 due on July 31. She invests £30,000 in an EIS fund on March 31 2012. She can carry back all tax relief due to 2011/12. That will generate a refund of £6,000 (£30,000 x 20%). And as her tax bill for 2011/12 has reduced by £6,000, her POAs for 2012/13 will follow suit, making a total reduction in the payments to the Taxman of £12,000. That's 40% of the sum she invested.

Solution

Making an investment into an Enterprise Investment Scheme by April 5 2013 can cut your self-assessment tax payments by 40% of the amount invested. But half of this saving is temporary and will be repayable with your self-assessment payment in January 2014.

36. Using a bond to skip higher tax rates

Problem

The tax year 2010/11 saw the introduction of the 50% rate; this will reduce to 45% from April 6 2013, but it looks like this higher rate will be with us for some time to come. But assuming that tax rates will fall in future, is there a way to ride out the higher rate storm until that time comes?

What are investment bonds?

Investment bonds (IBs) have been around for decades but have attracted new interest since the increase in income tax rates was announced. IBs are mainly marketed by life assurance companies. Usually, your investment will need to be a single lump sum payment that the insurance company will place in a fund of your choice. There are hundreds of different funds on offer from Asian developing markets to UK property funds. In that sense an IB is similar to other investments like unit trusts. But what makes it unique is the way in which the profit from the bond is taxed.

There are three main factors that make the taxation of IBs advantageous:

- no tax is payable until you draw income from the bond or cash it in, fully or partly. This is in contrast with, say, stocks and shares, or even deposit accounts where dividends or interest are paid out regularly whether you like it or not, and, of course, it's subjected to tax

- you can draw up to 5% of your investment tax-free for each year, up to a maximum of 20 years

- the profit the bond makes will only be taxed when you surrender (cash-in) some or all of it.

> ### TIP
> You can take the tax-free 5% however you like, for example in monthly instalments. So, for instance, if you invested £60,000 into a bond, you could draw £250 a month (that's equal to £3,000 per year) for up to 20 years; or you could take nothing for 24 months and then take £6,000 tax-free all at once.

Trap. If the IB doesn't generate 5% profit each year, taking that amount means that you're eating into the capital you originally invested. If you don't want to do that, then reduce what you draw to match the growth as near as possible.

6

How to skip higher rate tax

You can decide when to surrender the bond and so when tax will have to be paid on the profit it makes; you can wait up to 20 years for the tax rates to drop again. In the meantime you can draw up to 5% of your investment tax-free each year.

Example

Rob invested £60,000 into an IB in April 2010. He immediately started to draw £250 per month tax-free. The government decides to drop tax rates back to 40% in 2016/17. So in April 2016 Rob surrenders the bond for £60,500. He has to pay tax on the profit it made of £18,500, i.e. Rob invested £60,000 and has drawn 72 monthly payments of £250 each (£18,000). The bond is worth £500 more in April 2016 than Rob paid for it, so in total he's gained £18,500. He'll pay 40% tax on this, whereas if the profit had been taxable in the years between April 2010 and 2016, he would have paid 50% or 45%. Rob has saved himself around £1,300 tax.

Solution

Use an investment bond to dodge the 50%/45% or 60% tax rates. You can make a single lump sum investment and draw out 5% of this amount as tax-free income for up to 20 years. You'll only be taxed on any profit the IB makes when you cash it in. So if tax rates have dropped back to their previous levels by then, you will have skipped the current 50%/45% and 60% tax rates.

37. Higher tax rate avoidance

Problem

In recent years the government has introduced a range of changes to increase tax for those they consider to have "high incomes". The new rules are designed to hide some of the extra charges. How can you use these rules to work in your favour?

Tax rates

For 2012/13, taxable income up to £34,370 is charged at 20%, over that and the rate climbs to 40%. The next increase hits when your income reaches the £100,000 mark when the tax rate peaks at 60%, and for income over £150,000 the tax rate is 50%.

Gifting to save tax

Payments under the Gift Aid scheme entitle you to reduce your tax bill if you pay at higher rates. For example, £80 paid to a charity will get you a reduction in your tax bill of between £20 and £40. But if you pay basic rate tax, there will be no reduction. Therefore, while there's no financial gain in making extra Gift Aid payments just to get the higher tax relief, you should aim to get the maximum tax relief on payments you do make.

TIP

If you pay tax at a higher rate than your partner, then you should make all the Gift Aid payments and vice versa.

TIP

With school holidays always just around the corner it's worth looking out for visitor attractions that allow you to pay the entrance fee by Gift Aid, such as zoos, museums, or annual passes for the National Trust. Don't forget to include these on your tax return so that you get the extra tax relief.

Pension premiums

Pension contributions can also offer married couples a chance for tax planning. Although you and your spouse may both work and pay your own pension premiums, there's no tax reason why you can't reorganise these in a similar way to the Gift Aid payments.

The spouse who pays the lower rate of tax can give up paying their pension contributions and the higher rate taxpayer can pay a similar amount into their own fund. This can produce a substantial tax saving overall.

Example

Phil's taxable annual income, after deducting pension premiums of £10,000, is £110,000. He pays 60% tax on £10,000 of his income and 40% on the rest. Julie has taxable income of £30,000 per year after pension premiums of £5,000. Julie gets tax relief of £1,000, i.e. 20%, on her pension payments. If she gave up making these and Phil increased his contributions by the same amount, he would get tax relief of £3,000, i.e. at 60%. That's a £2,000 tax saving per year.

Trap. Stopping payment of your premiums can affect the terms of your policy. Therefore, before going ahead with this strategy you should check the consequences with your pensions advisor.

Solution

Where your partner's income tax rate differs from yours, maximise the tax relief on Gift Aid payments and pension premiums by ensuring that these are made only by the one paying the highest rate of tax. This can save up to 40p tax in the pound; for example, paying a pension premium of £5,000 can save £2,000 tax.

38. Shift income without shifting the asset

Problem

Where you own an asset which produces income, you'll be taxed on this at your highest rate. If you want to shift the income to your spouse who pays tax at a lower rate than you, you have to transfer the asset into their name, which you may not want to do.

Independent taxation

The Taxman's rules say that married couples are taxed on income from their jointly owned investments on a 50/50 basis. This means, for example, if you own 25% of a property that you rent out and your spouse owns the other 75%, the Taxman will expect you to each pay tax on 50% of the income. If you pay tax at different rates, this can be a problem.

Form 17

If you and your spouse own an asset in unequal proportions and you want the income you get from it to be taxed in line with your share (i.e. not 50/50), you need to make a special tax election. This is done by submitting a Form 17 to the Taxman (see the Appendix for a weblink). You don't have to make an election if you don't want to, you can carry on being taxed on a 50/50 basis for as long as you like and then submit an election if and when you want to switch to being taxed on the actual share of the income.

Special rules for married couples

Just to complicate matters, there are some exceptions to these special rules for married couples.

Trap 1. No matter how you share interest earned from a joint bank account, the Taxman says it must be taxed 50/50. So Form 17 is not applicable in relation to such accounts.

Trap 2. An election is not required for dividends from jointly-owned shares in a "close company", i.e. one controlled by five or fewer people; these will be taxed in proportion to ownership anyway.

Making the rules work for you

With some simple planning the Taxman's rules can be turned to your advantage. If you are liable to the 50% plus tax rates that apply from 2010/11 but your spouse isn't, shifting some of your investment income to them seems like a good idea. But you may not want to give up ownership of the asset.

TIP

Transferring just a small share of an asset, say 5%, into your spouse's name can actually shift 50% of the income to them, but only for tax purposes.

TIP

Just putting a bank account into joint names will mean each spouse will be taxed on 50% of the interest it produces.

Example

Jane's portfolio of shares pays dividends of £18,000 per year. Her salary will be £90,000 in 2012/13 and she'll have to pay 60% tax on her income over £100,000. Peter, her husband, earns the same salary but has investment income of just a few pounds. Jane gifts a 5% interest in all of her shares to Peter but they don't make an election on Form 17. This means that 50% of the dividends will be taxed on him. Both their incomes will now be below £100,000 and so they will escape the 60% tax rate entirely, saving £1,600.

Solution

Transferring a small share of an asset, say 5%, into your spouse's name will make them liable to tax on 50% of the income but it means you keep possession of most of the asset. If you pay higher rate tax but your spouse doesn't, this is an easy way to shift income and so reduce your tax bill.

SECTION 7

Pensions

In one form or another, pensions have been at the centre of tax changes over the last 25 years. Successive governments have attacked the tax-free status of money in your pension fund and aimed to restrict the amount of tax relief you can claim on contributions.

Now, more than ever, you need to know how to maximise the remaining tax breaks on offer. Whether it's negotiating the tricky contribution rules or funding alternatives, this section provides some invaluable ideas.

39. Arrears of pension contributions

Problem

Your pension advisor has said that your company can claim full tax relief on all pension contributions paid on behalf of your spouse, but what's the maximum it can pay?

Remuneration package

You've heard of directors taking small salaries but getting their company to pay massive pension contributions on their behalf. As long as their overall remuneration package is reasonable for the work they do, an employee/director can legitimately split their salary and pension contribution in whatever proportions they wish and they will count as a tax deductible cost for the company.

However, it's worth noting the Taxman's view regarding employee close relatives. His instructions **(BIM 46035)** say that a pension contribution is deductible *"If the pension contribution paid on behalf of such directors or employees is the same as that paid for a third party employee in similar circumstances you can accept that there is no non-business purpose and allow a deduction for the full amount of the contribution."* (For a weblink to BIM 46035 see the Appendix.)

Example

John is a director of a small company and employs his spouse for general administration work. A modest salary of £1,200 a year is paid, which is easily commensurate with the duties she carries out. The company also pays an employer's contribution into a personal pension scheme for her of £100 per month.

John's pension advisor is insisting that the company is perfectly entitled to full tax relief on all of the £1,200 annual contributions and can actually pay up to the £3,600 annual maximum. This is because the pension rules say that even where someone has no taxable income they are entitled to income tax relief on pension premiums of up to £3,600. But the rules for personal tax relief differ from those for companies. For a company to claim relief it has to justify that the pension contributions have a genuine business motive. In other words, that the pension contributions paid on behalf of an employee are appropriate and reasonable in respect of the job they do.

TIP

You can justify the current pension contribution by taking into account the number of years of service, and salary paid in those years, before your company decided to pay pension contributions. So, for example, if you had employed your spouse for five years and only just decided to start paying pension contributions on their behalf, you could look back and add up the amounts which could be justified for those earlier years.

TIP

You can also justify a "one off" company pension contribution for your spouse to a year of higher profits and record them as a reward for helping to earn those profits. This should pass the Taxman's test for tax deductibility.

Solution

Your company can make regular pension contributions for your spouse as long as it's at a similar rate to what other employees might receive and it relates to making up for past years' service. Or as a one-off you could pay a performance-related contribution.

40. Transferring property as pension premiums

Problem

Your financial advisor has suggested transferring the company offices into your pension fund to bump up its value and save tax. It sounds like a great idea but a colleague has told you it could trigger a big tax bill for the company.

The plan

The idea is simple enough: your company can transfer a share, or maybe all, of the property it occupies into your pension fund. The value of the transfer will be treated as a pension contribution on your behalf. Once transferred, your company will pay rent to your pension fund for use of the building. The rent will be deductible from the company's Corporation Tax (CT) bill. And, better still, your pension fund won't have to pay a penny in tax on the rent because it has tax-exempt status.

Exit strategy

Where the property is worth more now than was paid for it, the increase is treated as a tax chargeable gain when the company transfers all or part of it into your pension fund.

Example - part 1

Simon is the only director/shareholder of SD Ltd. The company operates its business from offices which it bought for £115,000 eight years ago. They're now worth £150,000. SD transfers the building into Simon's pension fund and, as a result, the £45,000 increase in value becomes chargeable to CT. Even though SD is allowed to reduce the gain to take account of inflation since it bought the property (this is called indexation), it will still have a CT bill. Assuming the company pays tax at the lower rate of 20%, the CT on the gain will be around £6,000. At this point you may be thinking twice about the idea, but there's some more good news.

Corporation Tax deduction

As the transfer of the property is treated as a pension contribution, the company can claim a CT deduction for it.

Example - part 2

The transfer of the property by SD is treated as a pension contribution for Simon and is therefore tax deductible. So SD can claim relief on the whole £150,000 giving it a reduction in its CT bill of £30,000 (£150,000 x 20%). Thus the spectre of £6,000 CT payable has been turned into a £29,000 (£35,000 - £6,000) tax windfall for SD. Not only that but Simon's pension fund now owns a property earning tax-free rent. And, just to top it off, its tax-exempt status means that any gain it makes when it sells the property is also tax-free.

Note. The limit on tax deductible pension contributions you and your employer can make together is £50,000. But where this limit hasn't been used in full in the previous three years it can be brought forward to increase the current year's limit.

Transfer in practice

While all the figures here stack up to a very tax-efficient way to extract income and capital from your company, it's complex and not a DIY process.

TIP

Use a pension fund manager that specialises in transferring commercial property into a personal pension fund (see the Appendix for weblinks to pension companies that specialise in commercial property). There are significant costs, but as an overall tax-saving scheme they don't come much better.

Solution

Transferring your company's premises into your pension fund may trigger a Corporation Tax (CT) bill. But it can claim a tax deduction which could mean an overall CT saving. Rent from the property will be tax-exempt, as will any gain when the property is sold. However, the initial costs of this scheme are high.

41. Transferring assets to your pension fund

Problem

The decline in the stock market may have cut the value of your investments and your pension fund. How can you turn this tragedy to your advantage and receive tax-free cash in the process?

Background

If you make a contribution to a registered pension scheme, both you and the pension fund get a tax break, but does the current economic climate offer you an unexpected advantage?

Age benefit

Once you're over the retirement age for your pension scheme you can draw 25% of the fund as a tax-free lump sum. Your scheme's retirement age could be as low as 50 if you were born before April 6 1960. Those younger need to reach at least 55 before drawing a tax-free lump sum.

Example

Tony is aged 55, i.e. over the retirement age for his pension scheme, and earns £150,000 in 2012/13. The value of his share portfolio has crashed from £160,000 to £120,000, so he sells it all and reinvests the proceeds in his pension scheme. The cash effect for Tony and his pension scheme is as follows:

PENSION FUND RECEIVES:	£
Net contribution from Tony	120,000
Tax reclaimed by fund managers	30,000
Total received by fund	150,000
TONY RECEIVES:	
Tax-free cash draw-down	37,500
Tax relief at 20%	24,000
Total cash received	61,500
Less loss on share sales	(40,000)
Tony's net cash position	21,500

NOTE. The limit on pension contributions that qualify for tax relief is £50,000 per year. But where the contributions have been less than this limit, the unused part can be carried forward up to three years and added to the limit for a later year.

An alternative approach

Brian is in the same position as Tony but he optimistically believes the stock market will recover, so he doesn't want to sell his share portfolio. However, he also needs to boost the value of his pension fund as he wants to retire in ten years' time. Brian decides to transfer his shares directly into his Self-Invested Pension Plan (SIPP) as an "in specie" contribution.

Brian's cash position is almost the same as Tony's because the transfer of his shares to the SIPP is treated as a sale for tax purposes. The difference is that the pension trustees must pay Stamp Duty of £750 (£150,000 x 0.5%) on the acquisition of the shares, which will reduce the fund value slightly.

Advantages of SIPPs

Brian can make a transfer of his shares directly to his pension scheme as it's a self-invested scheme, which means he has some control over what it invests in. This would not be possible with a standard personal pension scheme.

Once the shares are inside the SIPP, any increase in their value is protected from Capital Gains Tax (CGT). Brian has also retained control over his share portfolio and he will continue to benefit from its growth in value.

TIP

Open market assets such as quoted shares should be accepted without valuation as a transfer in specie by the pension fund trustees.

TIP

You can transfer a wide range of assets into a SIPP, including unquoted shares and non-residential property. (For further information on SIPPs and in specie transfers into them see the Appendix.)

Solution

Transfer assets to your SIPP while their values are depressed; this can mean you could pay little or no CGT and future growth will be tax-free. You will also receive tax relief on the value transferred.

42. Using your company as your pension fund

Problem

Tax relief on pension contributions is tightly controlled, as are the sort of investments you can make with your pension fund. How can you increase the amount you can set aside for retirement and have more control over what you invest your pension fund in?

Retiring from business

Companies are generally considered to be a tax efficient vehicle to run your business through. But when you're ready to sell up or retire, it can be difficult to decide on the best strategy to get your money out of the company.

Options

Ideally, you could sell your shares to another company or individual. The profit/gain you made from the deal would be chargeable to Capital Gains Tax (CGT). Alternatively, you could wind the company up and transfer the money and assets into your own name. This would also be a capital transaction and taxable under the CGT rules. In either situation you could claim entrepreneurs' relief (ER) on the gain and benefit from a tax rate of just 10%.

Example

John is the only shareholder in J Ltd, a trading company. He started the company with just £100 as share capital. In July 2012 he retires and sells the company to a competitor for £818,280. After deducting his CGT exemption (£10,600) the gain of £807,580 is subject to CGT at the ER rate of just 10%. So John ends up with a CGT bill of £80,758, i.e. 10% of the chargeable gain.

Taking dividends

Alternatively, John could extract all the value by taking it as a dividend, leaving only his original £100 share capital, and then winding the company up. Assuming John's tax-free personal allowances have been used up for the year but he has all his basic rate band available, he would be faced with a personal tax bill of £280,847 (see the Appendix for a calculation of this figure). That's well over double the amount compared to taking a capital distribution.

Changing tax rates

John may have been a higher rate taxpayer while he was working but now he's retired he has little other money apart from the capital built up in his company. If he keeps the company running and drip-feeds dividends for as long as the capital lasts, he could extract all his money without paying a single penny more in tax.

Example

If John's other income, e.g. pensions and investments, was £15,000 per year, then using current levels of tax-free allowances and rate bands he could take a dividend of up to £24,728 a year without triggering a tax bill. It would bring his total income to £42,475 (see the note below). After taking off £8,105 personal tax-free allowances this would leave £34,370. As this doesn't exceed the basic rate band for 2011/12 of £35,000, it means John would have no tax on the dividend to pay.

NOTE. A dividend of £24,728 is treated by the Taxman as gross income before tax of £27,475 because he treats the £24,728 as net of a 10% tax deduction, known as a tax credit.

TIP

As the tax-free allowances and basic rate bands increase each year, John can also increase his dividends to match.

TIP

If John had a spouse with a basic rate band to spare, he could transfer some of his shares to them and they too could draw tax-free dividends.

Conclusion. Don't rush to sell or wind up a company to get the 10% ER rate; consider keeping it alive and paying dividends within the basic rate band. This can produce a 0% tax rate.

Solution

When you retire, instead of taking all the value from your company extract the value by way of dividends over a number of years so that your taxable income for each year is less than the basic rate band. This would mean there would be no tax to pay on the money you take from the company. You can also transfer shares to your spouse so they too could draw dividends without further tax to pay.

SECTION 8

Profit extraction

Being in business is all about making profits, but when you do this through a company the trick is to get the money into your hands without triggering a massive tax and NI bill.

For example, you don't have to pay NI on dividends but you do on salary. But saving NI isn't the whole story. This section gives you a range of ideas on how to extract profit from your company in the most tax-efficient ways.

43. Tax-free benefits - as long as you're not close family

Problem

There are plenty of tax planning opportunities for family companies, but if you haven't tied the knot, how can you get tax-free benefits for your partner?

Shifting benefits

The Taxman puts particular effort into blocking directors and company owners from getting their money out of the business by shifting income to their spouse or other family members.

Spouse tax benefits-in-kind trap

Providing your spouse with benefits-in-kind (BiK) from your company might appear to be an obvious tax-saving strategy: if they aren't employed, then you might think that they can't be taxable on employment-related benefits.

Trap. The Taxman has this covered with s.201 of the **Income Tax (Employment and Pensions) Act 2003** (ITEPA), which says that a BiK is taxable on the director/employee where it's provided to *"a member of an employee's family or household".* For BiK purposes, anyone who is financially dependent on you is treated as part of your family.

Not related

Logically the "family trap" doesn't apply to company directors/shareholders who are unmarried. But while a financially independent unmarried partner doesn't count as family, s.201 of ITEPA might still catch you for a tax charge if they are a member of your "household". ITEPA says that household includes domestic staff or guests. So as long as they aren't your butler etc. and you share living expenses as well as each owning part of your home, or share the rent, the Taxman can't argue that they are your guest.

Profit extraction

Not associated

If yours is a close company, that means one that's controlled by five or fewer people, a BiK given to you or someone "associated" with you will be subject to a tax charge. "Associate" has a specific definition for tax. It means: spouse, parent, grandparent, great-grandparent etc., children, grandchildren etc., brother or sister, and business partner. But there's no mention of nephews, nieces, cousins, fiancées, or live-in partners.

Tax-free benefits

Despite the Taxman's anti-avoidance rules for BiKs that apply to family and household guests and associates, your company can, for example, pay a mobile phone contract or medical insurance premium for your live-in partner and there will be no tax or NI charge. This tax break can also be used for nephews or nieces who you think deserve a tax-free perk for their birthday.

TIP

Whatever the BiK you choose, the purchase should be directly between your company and the supplier to avoid any suggestion by the Taxman that it's a purchase on your behalf and so taxable.

Trap. Your company won't get a Corporation Tax deduction for the costs of the BiK. But the personal tax saving should outweigh this loss.

Solution

Your company can provide tax and NI-free BiKs to your unmarried partner (as long as they're financially independent), or even cousins, nephews and nieces. The purchase must be made directly by your company from the supplier or it could be taxed.

44. Spouse's pension

Problem

If your spouse is an employee of your company, pension contributions can be paid for them. However, to obtain a tax deduction for these you might need to justify that it qualifies as a business expense.

Profit extraction

You might already be using the tax-free personal allowance to its full advantage by getting the company to pay your spouse/partner a tax and NI-free salary of, say, £6,400, either spread over the year or by planning a one-off bonus just before the end of the tax year. But there is another opportunity to extract more tax-free income from the company using pension schemes.

Your company can pay into any employee's personal pension plan without it being treated as income for tax purposes. This makes it a particularly good way to reward employees, including your spouse, with tax and NI-free earnings.

Justifiable business expense

The basic rule is that only expenses which are wholly and exclusively for the business can be deducted from profits for tax purposes. The Taxman has always targeted the payment of spouse's wages or salary where these appear to be more than would be paid to an unconnected employee doing the same job.

For example, where your company pays your spouse an annual salary of £11,400, and the Taxman argues that the justifiable salary package for a job is only £7,000, then the adjustment he will seek to disallow is £4,400 of this, even where this has been paid in the form of a pension contribution for your spouse.

Rate of pay

A total package of £11,650 works out at just over 37 hours a week at the National Minimum Wage (NMW) rate of £6.08 (£6.19 from October 1 2012) per hour, over 52 weeks. However, your spouse's rate per hour might actually be higher than this.

Your response

The Taxman's own technical guide says that his inspectors are supposed to consider the total paid to the spouse; it's not appropriate to deal with the pension separately. This means he can't target the pension premium for disallowance just because it happens to be the most tax-efficient part of the salary package you pay your spouse.

TIP

It's difficult for anyone to say exactly how much an employee should be paid, not even the Taxman. This means there's plenty of scope for argument. Provide the Taxman with the calculations that justify your spouse's total package and let him try to knock it down.

Download Zone

For a **Spouse's Job Description**, visit **http://books.indicator.co.uk**. You'll find the access code on page 2 of this book.

Solution

As long as it's reasonable and in line with the work they do, you can pay your spouse or partner any rate of remuneration you like, including part of it as a pension premium directly into their fund. The cost to your company of your spouse's wages and pension contributions count as a business expense.

45. Making use of personal losses in a company

Problem

The hobby that turned into a small business unfortunately never took off. In fact, so far it's made a small loss and left you stuck with some hardly-used equipment. Can you claim a tax deduction for this?

Losing losses

If a business makes a loss, the Taxman allows you to deduct it from your other income and so reduce your tax bill. At first sight the rules appear generous, allowing carry forward, carry back and even sideways loss relief. But as you would expect, the Taxman applies lots of conditions. One is that if your business ceases and you haven't been able to get tax relief for all your losses, he won't let you carry them forward to another business.

Company income

You might have started off as a sole trader or partnership which made a loss but when trade improved you formed a company leaving yourself with some losses from the "old business" on which you couldn't get tax relief. Your accountant told you it was tough luck. But actually, as the company is carrying on the original trade, s.86 of the **Income Taxes Act 2007** allows you to transfer the loss from the unincorporated business against income you take from the company.

Example

Joe started a motor workshop in 2008. It had high set-up costs and initially trade was slow. This meant that the business made losses of £40,000 during its first two years. But trading improved considerably and Joe's accountant recommended that he incorporate the business. Joe transferred the trade to a company. In the tax year 2011/12 Joe paid himself a salary of £40,000 to use up his losses from the old business. He would normally pay tax on this of around £6,500; instead, he'll pay no tax at all. And if the company can't afford to pay him all the salary at once, he can leave it in his director's loan account and draw down on the tax-free funds whenever he wants to.

Subject to the following conditions you can draw tax-free salary or dividends from the company by using the loss from the unincorporated business:

- the business must have been transferred mainly in exchange for shares in the company. HMRC will accept that 80% or more is sufficient to meet this test. The 80% refers to the net value of the company

- the person claiming the loss relief must own the shares given in exchange for the unincorporated business

- the company must carry on the business throughout the entire tax year in which the loss is claimed.

Tax losses and hobbies

There's another angle to the pre-incorporation tax break. If, as well as your company, you or your spouse has a hobby business that's making a loss, you can also use s.86.

Transfer your loss-making part-time business into your company. Provided it continues the trade, you, or your spouse if it's their business, can use the loss to extract tax-free salary. Once the losses have been used up the company can simply close down the hobby trade if it's still not viable.

This scheme will work whether the business being transferred into your company is yours or your spouse's. But check whether sideways loss relief is available first, as this is easier to claim.

Sideways loss relief involves setting the losses against other income you received in the year the business made the loss, or the previous year. A claim can be made in writing at any time, or you can just include it on your tax return.

HMRC's **Help Sheet HS227 "Losses"** explains the procedure for claiming tax relief on losses. (For a weblink to this Help Sheet see the Appendix.)

Trap. You can only use the s.86 tax break where you run your hobby business with the intention of making a profit. If it's purely for pleasure, the Taxman says you can't claim tax relief for losses. On the plus side though, he won't charge tax if you occasionally make a profit, but that's another story.

Solution

Transfer the trade of a loss-making unincorporated business into a company and use it to get tax-free salary or dividends. This could, for example, save £6,500 on a salary of £40,000. You can use the same strategy for your hobby business if it makes a loss, but if sideways loss relief is available, i.e. relief for setting the loss against tax you've paid on other income in the same year, claim this in preference.

8

Profit extraction

46. Repaying share capital

Problem

You have substantial funds tied up in your company as share capital. Is there an easy way you can release some of this and make use of the cash in a tax effective way?

Change in procedure

Until October 2009 if you wanted to reduce your company's share capital, it was necessary to apply to the High Court for clearance. However, a change in company law allows this to be achieved with a more simple procedure that doesn't require court clearance (see the Appendix for more information on share capital).

Tax consequences

The return of share capital will usually be a non-taxable event, but where the repayment is effectively a distribution of profit, you might have to pay tax on it as if it were income.

Tax may be due where a further reorganisation of share capital takes place, typically the issue of bonus shares, either before of after the repayment of share capital that is linked to it. In these circumstances it is treated as a distribution of profits chargeable to tax like a dividend.

Reasons to repay share capital

If your company no longer relies on the share capital to fund its operations, then releasing it will, at the very least, provide you with some tax-free cash. But what can you then do with the money?

TIP

You could loan the money back to the company and charge interest. Like dividends, this would not be liable to NI. The advantage of a loan compared with share capital is that the terms, e.g. interest rates, can be different for each lender. Should one or more shareholders want to take their windfall and spend it on a new car, that's fine.

Director's loan account

If you have borrowed money from the company and have an overdrawn loan account, there can be consequential tax charges and the Taxman is particularly keen in targeting these. If the loan account is sufficiently overdrawn, £5,000 for a director and £15,000 for a company, there will be tax to pay for both.

TIP

If you borrowed from your company and this has given rise to tax charges, you could use the money from the repayment of share capital to repay the loan and so cut the tax bill for you and your company.

Income shifting

Although the Taxman has deferred the introduction of his anti-avoidance rules on income shifting, it pays to keep one step ahead as it seems certain that legislation will be introduced sometime in the foreseeable future.

One of the Taxman's big concerns is the payment of dividends to a spouse who takes little or no active role in the company's trade. However, the Taxman is not concerned with interest paid to a spouse on a loan they made to the company, provided it's made on commercial terms. This means you can't charge an excessive amount of interest.

TIP

Your company could repay share capital to you, and your spouse if they also have shares, and the money used to fund a loan from your spouse to the company. The interest paid to them should not be considered as income shifting by the Taxman.

Solution

If your company repays share capital to you, it's not usually taxable. It can be made more tax-efficient if you loan the money back to the company and charge it interest as this income isn't subject to NI charges. You might also use the funds to repay your overdrawn director's loan account and so avoid a tax charge on this.

47. Protecting your director's loan account from NI

Problem

Your company regularly pays your personal bills and recharges those costs to you via your director's loan account. This has never caused a problem with the Taxman in the past but now he's saying that you'll have to pay tax on it.

Regular costs

You take a modest monthly salary from your company and receive an annual dividend once the profit for the year is finalised. But when large bills crop up, such as car repairs or holidays, the company picks up the tab and charges the cost to your director's loan account. If this causes your loan account to slide into the red for a few months, it can result in a tax bill.

£5,000 loan limit

When your loan account goes overdrawn by more than £5,000, the Taxman says you are getting the benefit of an interest-free loan. You need to either pay interest on that loan at the official rate, currently 4%, or pay tax on that estimated interest.

Example

If your account is overdrawn by, say, £15,000 for six months, the interest due at the Taxman's official rate is £300 (£15,000 x 4% x 6/12). The tax payable at 40% amounts to £120 (£300 x 40%) - not much to worry about. However, the company is also stung with Class 1A NI at 13.8% on the estimated interest; this would be £41 (£300 x 13.8%) - again that won't break the bank.

Repaying the loan

Your accountant always sorts this out at the year-end, either by getting the company to vote you a bonus, or by allocating some of the annual dividend to your director's loan account. Either way the account is written back to zero and everyone's happy - except the Taxman.

Trap. The Taxman takes the view that any personal expenses charged to your loan account are advance payments of salary, so you and the company have to pay Class 1 NI at the time these amounts are credited to your loan account. Tax bill?

Example

The company paid your car repair bill of £3,500 on May 1 2012 and your holiday charge of £2,000 on June 1 2012. The NI due is:

BILL PAID:	NI DUE ON: (*)	EMPLOYERS' NI	EMPLOYEES' NI
£3,500 1/5/12	19/6/12	£483 (£3,500 x 13.8%)	£420 (£3,500 x 12%)
£2,000 1/6/12	19/7/12	£276 (£2,000 x 13.8%)	£240 (£2,000 x 12%)

The total NI cost becomes more material at £1,419.

Intention for borrowing

If your intention was always to clear the account with a dividend or personal funds, the expenses making up the overdrawn balance can't be earnings and are not subject to Class 1 NI.

TIP

If the Taxman refuses to agree with you, refer him to para 29 of his leaflet, **CA44: National Insurance for Company Directors**. This says that there's no liability for NI on the overdrawn amount, or the increase in the overdrawn amount, if the withdrawal is made in anticipation of an introduction of funds which are not earnings, for example, dividends, matured insurance policies or other personal income.

Solution

Get the company to minute its policy regarding overdrawn directors' accounts: that those accounts must be cleared by a dividend or personal funds introduced by the director, and are not intended to be advances on directors' salary due.

Profit extraction

8

48. Phased share buy backs

Problem

A company has the power to buy back its own shares from its shareholders, allowing you to cash in on your investment tax efficiently. But the deal has to meet certain conditions to qualify for maximum tax saving. How can you achieve this?

Exit route

Let's say you've had enough and want out of your company and would like someone to buy your shares. If the other shareholders are unable or unwilling to buy the shares, then your company could buy them instead. Of course, the company has to be able to afford to do this, both in terms of profits and cash. However, it can be done in instalments.

Substantial reduction test

Where you sell shares back to your company the money you receive will be treated as income, like a dividend, and taxed at rates of up to 42.5%. However, the Taxman will agree to treat the money as a capital payment and so subject to Capital Gains Tax, which means you may be taxed at as little as 10%. But the "substantial reduction test" must be passed for this to apply. After your shares have been bought back, your remaining interest in the company must not exceed 75% of your original interest. For example, where you originally held 100 ordinary shares in a company and it agreed to buy back 40 of these, the test would be passed as you'll only have 60% of your original shareholding remaining.

Trap. In determining your interest in the company the Taxman can include the shareholding etc. of your associates. For example, a husband and wife are associated persons and their shares must be combined when determining whether the interest in the company has been reduced. However, in the **Preston Meats Ltd** case (SpC 435) another solution was attempted.

Insufficient funds

Preston Meats did not have sufficient funds to buy back a departing director/shareholder's (Mr S's) ordinary shares, valued at £150,000.

Step 1. In order to fund the purchase the company issued 130,000 £1 redeemable interest-bearing preference shares, carrying no voting rights.

Step 2. The funds the company received for the preference shares were used to buy back and cancel Mr S's ordinary shares.

Step 3. In time the company would buy back (redeem) the preference shares issued, out of future trading profits. The phased redemption being: 30,000 shares after five years, another 50,000 after ten years had elapsed and the remainder at the 15-year stage.

The preference shares were to be purchased by Mr S's daughter. For the purposes of the substantial reduction test, she was not deemed to be their associate because her shares could not be aggregated with those of her parents, as she was over 18.

Tax advantage

Provided your shares have been held for at least five years, on a share buy-back you can usually choose between paying Capital Gains Tax (CGT) or income tax on the sale proceeds. However, with entrepreneurs' relief you can secure an effective CGT rate of at least 10%, compared to an effective rate of tax of 25% for an income distribution. CGT treatment is mandatory if certain conditions, e.g. the substantial reduction test, are met, so the Taxman can't overturn your choice.

Unfortunately, Mr S failed to pass the test because the preference share certificate was actually issued to him, and he had included the interest received on the shares on his annual tax returns. This all pointed to them being his shares, not his daughter's.

TIP

To fund a buy back, issue new redeemable shares. Avoid the substantial reduction problem by making sure the redeemable (preference) shares are issued to someone who is not associated with you, for CGT purposes.

TIP

Get advance clearance from the Taxman for the whole plan. And make sure you stick to exactly what you have told him in the clearance procedure.

Solution

Use a share buy-back to extract profits from your company. Fund this with an issue of redeemable preference shares to a new shareholder. They can be your son or daughter, provided they are over 18.

SECTION 9

Property

Whether it's a family home or a holiday cottage, for most people property represents one of their biggest investments. While you can usually expect few tax problems with your home, investment property is another matter.

In this section we've included plenty of pointers on how to stop the Taxman from taking such a big bite out of your property income or gains. So if you're renting out, or you want to sell or transfer a property, there's something here for you.

49. Tax-efficient allocation of property income

Problem

Supposing you and your spouse own a rental investment property in equal shares. As you pay income tax on your share of rents at the rate of 50% and your spouse at only 20%, there would certainly be a benefit to you as a couple if you could allocate a larger proportion to them each year. But is it possible to do this?

Taxman's conundrum

Understandably, the Taxman expects everyone to pay tax on their income and not pass it over to someone else to pay on simply because it will save money. And when it comes to income from investments, whether that's bank accounts, shares or a rental property, he expects you to declare and pay tax on the income in proportion to your ownership of the asset.

Change of ownership

The simple solution is that you can just transfer your share of the property to your spouse. This means that as they would then own all of the property they would pay the tax on all the income. This idea works but it's a bit cumbersome if you want to switch the income back later or just want to vary how much you each get from year to year. And there's also the matter of perhaps not wanting to transfer all your assets into your spouse's name.

Partnership arrangement

You can transfer the property to a Limited Liability Partnership (LLP). Strictly, this is closer to a company than a partnership in the way it's treated under general law. But the Taxman chooses to ignore general law in this case and treats an LLP like any ordinary partnership.

Partnerships can share profits between its partners in any way the partners want and entirely without regard to who owns the partnership assets. So you could easily vary the income between you and your spouse each and every year while retaining the 50/50 ownership.

Trap. There is one drawback though. LLPs have to submit accounts and an annual return to Companies House each year the same as a company does. The accounts must be in an approved format and so you may need an accountant to prepare these. If you keep good records this should cost no more than several hundred pounds, but you need to factor this in against any potential tax savings.

TIP

The property LLP tax-saving arrangement can work for others too with a different number of partners. But it would be advisable to speak to your accountant before pressing ahead. They will help you set up the LLP to get the most advantages for tax purposes and avoid any traps.

Solution

Use an LLP to hold a joint investment property. You can vary the income each partner is taxed on from year to year without having to change the ownership of the asset.

50. Getting property out of your company

Problem

You want to transfer your company's trading premises into your personal ownership but because you're taking value out of your company there will always be tax payable. How can you keep this to a minimum?

Paying the full price

The obvious way to acquire the property is to simply pay your company for it at its full market value. But unless you have cash available you'll need to raise a loan to do it, which is not necessarily an easy task these days. You'll also have to meet the loan repayments out of your taxed income; that is after PAYE tax and NI. Worse still, you'll also have to pay Stamp Duty Land Tax (SDLT) on the purchase price. On a property worth, say, £600,000 that's another £24,000 you'll be handing over to the Taxman.

Paying less than the full price

If you can't afford to pay the full market value, you can pay your company less for the property than it's worth but this will have tax consequences.

Trap. Where the amount you pay is below the full market price, the shortfall is taxable. So if the property were worth £600,000 and you could only raise a loan of £300,000, the difference of £300,000 would be taxed as if it were a dividend. This could land you with a tax bill of up to £108,000. Plus, you'll still have to pay SDLT based on the market value of the property and not the lower price you actually paid.

Example

	£
Distribution/dividend	300,000
Add tax credit: one-ninth of distribution	33,333
Taxable amount	333,333
Maximum income tax rate 42.5%	141,666
Less tax credit	33,333
Additional tax payable	108,333

Company loan option

Alternatively, you could agree to pay your company the full price, and just owe it the money. The trouble is that your company would have to pay tax equal to 25% of the debt. On a £600,000 property that's £150,000, although your company gets this back if you repay the money, meaning you're back to square one before you even consider the extra tax payable under the benefit-in-kind rules on beneficial loans.

TIP

Your company can transfer the property as an "in specie dividend" to you, i.e. transfer an asset to you rather than pay cash. The procedure for this is the same as that for a normal dividend except instead of paying cash, it transfers an asset. The paperwork for transferring is the same as if you were buying the property, meaning that you'll have full title to it, but as you're not paying for it or owing the company anything, no SDLT is payable. So using the facts from our earlier example, you'll save £24,000. And as an in specie dividend is like any other as far as the Taxman is concerned, there's no PAYE or NI to worry about.

Company tax bill

Although an in specie dividend will cost you and your company less in income tax, NI and SDLT, there are still significant tax costs that can arise when transferring a property into your own name. These are Corporation Tax in respect of any capital gain, and an additional rate tax charge on you for the higher rate tax on the dividend.

Solution

Use an "in specie" dividend to transfer a property from your company into your personal ownership. This is treated like a dividend so there's no PAYE tax or NI to pay and you'll also avoid Stamp Duty Land Tax.

51. Giving away your second home

Problem

You've owned a holiday cottage for many years, which you and your family visit for up to five weeks each year. The property originally cost £75,000 and is now worth £200,000. How do you transfer the property to your children without triggering a Capital Gains Tax (CGT) charge or an Inheritance Tax (IHT) bill?

IHT and CGT

Where you make a gift of property to anyone, including your children, there are two taxes which you need to consider: IHT and CGT. The good news is that Stamp Duty Land Tax doesn't apply where a property is transferred by way of a gift.

Using the figures mentioned above:

- it will take seven years before the gift is ignored for Inheritance Tax (IHT) purposes so there's a potential tax bill of £80,000 (£200,000 x 40% IHT); and

- there can be a Capital Gains Tax (CGT) charge of up to £35,000 (£125,000 at 28% CGT), without any proceeds from a sale to fund it. So this kind of generosity definitely has its downside.

Holiday business

If the property were to be commercially let as furnished holiday accommodation, then after two years it could be classed as business property for IHT purposes and would effectively be exempt from tax. On death, the property would pass to your beneficiaries free of IHT. There's no CGT on the transfer of the property, or any other asset, where it's transferred out of your estate on death, no matter how large the gain.

> **TIP**
>
> As an added bonus, renting the property should generate additional income, which can either supplement your own or be gifted away as surplus income (and therefore be ignored for IHT).

How is this achieved?

Trap. The property must be available to let for at least 210 days per year and let for at least 105 days. In addition, the property must not be let to one tenant for continuous periods over 31 days for more than 155 days in a year.

NOTE. The letting requirements require availability for 210 days and actual letting for 105 days; there is no need for these to be continuous or for the family to forego particular times. However, treat the 105-day letting and 210-day availability requirements as the bare minimum and not to friends and family.

Trap. To work this scheme requires that the letting is on a commercial basis with the aim of generating profits so that a few weeks letting at low rents to friends and family will not be sufficient. As a minimum, you should provide cleaning of the property and provision of clean linen with the house fully equipped for occupation.

TIP

Draw up a budget to show that you expect to make a profit and record explanations if results are below expectations. Keep records of the marketing of the property over the required period.

How about a buy-to-let?

The same tactic would also work with an existing buy-to-let property. This type of asset will also have a potential IHT problem.

You should consider changing the pattern of rentals to satisfy the holiday letting rules if possible, thereby enabling you to qualify for IHT business property relief. The rental of a property to tourists, such as short lets for a city flat, will exempt your property from IHT.

Solution

Leave the transfer of the property as part of your will. In the meantime, rent out your property as holiday accommodation. After just two years it will be free of IHT when you give it away. There's also no CGT liability on the increase in value of a property when it's gifted on death.

52. Using property rental losses

Problem

The tax rules that cover which expenses you can claim against property rental income are tough. They say that you can't deduct losses from your property rental income business from other types of income, e.g. salary. This means that the losses might be wasted.

Tax return basics

The accounting period for all rental income is the tax year, from April 6 to the following April 5. Each tax year you should prepare a rental income and expenditure account to establish whether or not you've made a profit. These accounts do not need to be submitted to the Taxman, but keep them for your own records and to help you complete the Land and Property pages on your tax return.

Losses problem

Unfortunately, it's not possible to offset these property losses against your other sources of income and so reduce your tax bill. Rental losses need to be set against a profit made on another property or must be carried forward to be set against future rental profits. So what you need is more rental profits from another property to get a tax deduction.

Renting your home

You can create rental income from your own home. By charging your company rent for providing office space at home you can generate income against which buy-to-let losses can be set. This means that you would be getting tax relief through your company for the rental losses you personally suffer on your buy-to-let property.

Will this be challenged?

When it comes to rent for a home office the Taxman will be looking for the existence of a formal rental agreement and *"regular independent rental valuations, carried out by a suitably qualified expert on a consistent basis"*. Indeed, failure to produce these may lead to the deduction for the expense in the company's records being disallowed. This rule can work to your advantage.

Download Zone

For a free sample **Rental Agreement**, visit **http://books.indicator.co.uk**. You'll find the access code on page 2 of this book.

TIP

As long as the amount of rent you charge the company is at market value, this is treated as income of your UK property business. If you want to do this, keep your rental charge in line with, say, local serviced office rentals; this should satisfy the Taxman's market value test.

TIP

Keep a note of the rental rates that local serviced offices charge, rather than engaging an independent rent valuer. Serviced office rental rates are generally inclusive of utilities and insurance so the comparison is reasonable. If your rental charge is in line with these figures, it will easily satisfy the market value test.

The Capital Gains Tax risk

In order to safeguard the CGT exemption on your main residence, make sure that you state in the agreement between you and the company that the facilities are only let to the company for a certain number of designated hours each week, e.g. 9am to 5pm Monday to Friday.

Solution

Where you make losses from renting out property but don't have other property rental profits against which you can set these, you can create additional rents by letting out a room in your house to your company. You can then offset this against your other property losses, which means you've generated a tax-free source of rental income.

53. Tax relief on capital expenses

Problem

For income tax purposes, property investment is treated as a business and, therefore, net rental income is calculated in the same way as profits from any other type of business. This means that you aren't allowed to claim a tax deduction for money you spend on capital items, e.g. equipment, in the same way as you can for running costs.

Working out your profit

The accounting period for all rental income is the tax year from April 6 to April 5. For each tax year, you need to prepare a rental income and expenditure account to establish whether or not you've made a profit. These accounts do not need to be sent to the Taxman but you should keep them for your own records and to help you complete the Land and Property pages on your tax return.

What can be claimed?

So-called "revenue expenses" are those costs that you incur during the day-to-day running of your property investment business and can be deducted from your rental income. Expenses that don't fall into this category will generally be capital costs which are dealt with in a different way.

Capital costs

Costs incurred in significantly improving your property are considered to be capital and can't be deducted. But you will usually be able to offset them against your capital gain when you sell the property. You need to keep a record of these by updating your schedule of capital costs each time you complete your rental accounts and tax return.

Smaller capital items

The Taxman expects the equipment and machinery that you purchase will be "wholly and exclusively" for managing your properties. For example, you may have bought equipment, such as a computer to record your rental income. More directly related to property management would be machinery for maintenance of the properties such as a vacuum cleaner, ladder, plumbing tools, carpet washer, drill and power washer.

The tax relief claimed on this type of item is known as capital allowances. The percentage rate of such allowances has tended to change on a regular basis during recent years. For your 2011/12 tax return you can claim 100% capital allowances on small capital items up to a maximum of £100,000. Expenditure above this level can be claimed at a rate of 20% per annum on the reducing balance basis.

Note. Since April 6 2012 the maximum amount of the 100% claim is to be reduced to £25,000 with the claim on any excess expenditure being reduced to 18%.

TIP

For equipment bought in 2011/12 up to the annual limit, claim 100% of the cost on the Land and Property pages of your 2011/12 tax return. However, you will need to keep a detailed note of the equipment bought, as this will probably have to be put in a separate box on the same return form.

Warning. For equipment inside the residential property, claim the wear and tear allowance or the renewal cost instead.

Solution

There's a window of opportunity for getting a full tax deduction for capital expenses, e.g. equipment, in your property rental business. Where you incurred the cost during 2011/12, you can claim 100% of the cost, up to a maximum of £100,000; thereafter this limit will be reduced to £25,000.

SECTION 10

Remuneration

PAYE tax and NI on employment income represents a huge slice of the UK's overall tax take, which is why the Taxman keeps such a tight grip on it. But there are still plenty of loopholes to take advantage of.

Whether you're paying your staff or yourself, in this section you'll find a wide range of tax-saving tips that you can use: from shifting income to avoiding higher or additional rate taxes to keeping staff costs down through the use of tax-free payments.

54. Keep your tax rate down to 10%

Problem

Most know about the tax rates of 20%, 40% and 50% but relatively few are aware of a 10% tax rate that still exits for savings income and dividends of up to £35,000. But how can you make use of this lower rate?

What counts as savings?

Savings income is, for example, interest paid by banks and building societies, whereas non-savings income is for most people wages or salaries, benefits-in-kind, pensions, profits from business and rental income.

Basic rate objective - mark one

Let's say, with the objective of staying within the basic rate tax band for 2012/13, you plan to restrict your total income for this coming year to £42,475. This will consist of, say, £13,000 salary, £27,000 dividend (that's £24,300 paid to you plus dividend tax credit) from your company, and £2,710 of bank interest (£2,168 plus tax of 20% deducted by the bank).

Your personal allowance is deducted from your salary first leaving you with taxable income of:

- non-savings of £4,895 (£13,000 - £8,105) taxed at 20%
- savings income of £2,710 taxed at 20%; and
- dividends of £27,000 taxed at 10%.

Apart from the tax paid at source you'll have further to pay of £979 (£4,895 x 20%) relating to the non-savings income. The tax deducted, or treated as deducted, at source from the savings income and dividends means that there's nothing further for you to pay on these.

> ## TIP
>
> You can actually convert this tax bill of £979 into a tax refund of £271 by altering the mix of income you take out of your company. Reduce your salary so it is just covered by your personal allowance of £8,105 and take the cash you need in the form of dividends. Also aim to keep your savings income to the savings income band of £2,710.

Basic rate objective - mark two

Your total income is still £42,475 but is now made up of: £8,105 salary and £31,660 (£34,370 - £2,710) dividends plus £2,710 gross (£2,168 net) interest.

Your tax-free personal allowance of £8,105 covers your salary, leaving nothing taxable. The gross interest falls within the savings income band of £2,710, so is taxed at 10%. Your taxable income after allowances amounts to £34,370 (£31,660 + £2,710), which is within the £34,370 limit for higher rate tax, so all of your dividend and savings income is taxed at 10% - the result you want!

Actually, a refund

After setting off the dividend tax credit of £3,166 and the 20% tax of £542 deducted by your bank from your interest, you are due a tax repayment of £271 - via your tax return for 2012/13.

TIP

You can keep your savings income within the savings band of £2,710 by transferring some of the interest-bearing funds to an account in your spouse's name. However, this will only save tax if your spouse is also taxed at the 10% rate.

Warning. Check the value of any benefits-in-kind your company provides, such as a company car or health insurance. These benefits are taxed alongside your salary so may use up the entire savings band of £2,710, pushing your savings income out of the 10% and into the 20% band.

Solution

Restrict your total salary and benefits to £8,105 in 2012/13 so the rest of your savings and dividend income is taxed at only 10%. You can even recover some of the tax you've paid at source on your bank interest.

55. Tax relief for your personal helper

Problem

Paying your spouse or partner's wage from your company is a well-established tax-saving arrangement. However, sometimes it's not possible or desirable to do this. Is there an alternative way to put them on the payroll and cut your tax bill?

Paying your partner

It's usually a good idea for your company to pay your spouse or partner as a way to reduce your tax bill. And as long as it's a bona fide job they're doing for the business, the Taxman doesn't have a problem with it either. Your company will be allowed to deduct the expense as a cost and you will be able to benefit by using both tax-free allowances against your household income.

Unfortunately, there are some situations in which it's not possible to take on your spouse as an employee. For example, it may require approval by your fellow directors or perhaps your company is making a loss and you don't want to make the accounts look worse than they are already. But there's still a way to pay your other half and claim a tax deduction, all without costing the company a penny.

Employees' expenses

There exists a little known tax break that allows employees and directors to claim a deduction for the cost of an assistant to help them do their job. The Taxman may not be too keen on this, but there's plenty of support for the idea. For a start, s.336 of the Income **Tax (Earnings and Pensions) Act 2003** that deals with employment expenses doesn't prevent it and the Taxman's own manual at **EIM32415** confirms that it's OK (see Appendix for a weblink).

However, even with the law on your side the rules for claiming employment expenses remain somewhat tricky to understand. But the Taxman's guidance once again comes to the rescue: it says he'll allow a claim where the duties of your job require you to employ and pay an assistant.

> **Tip**
>
> Amend your employment contract - identify existing aspects of your job that could be done by someone else. Add a clause to your director's service agreement which says that you must ensure the work specified is done and that it's your "duty" to employ an assistant to do it.

The duties you identify for your other half must be genuine and necessary for the proper completion of your own job, but apart from this condition they can be anything; secretarial help, bookkeeping, market research, telesales etc. The list may not be endless but if you put your thinking cap on it shouldn't be too difficult to come up with some specific duties which you can appoint your spouse or partner to assist you with.

Trap. As an employer you would need to run your own payroll and have to pay NI at 13.8% on anything you pay your assistant above the lower NI threshold, currently £139 per week. So aim to tailor the duties and pay to stay within the limit. Even at this level, assuming you pay income tax at 50%, and they have no other income, this will knock £3,614 (£139 x 52 x 50%) off your tax bill.

Solution

A tax break is available for directors and employees to claim a deduction for paying an assistant, which could be your spouse or partner, to help with your job. Add a clause to your contract stating what specific duties they'll do and that it's your job to employ someone to do them. Keep the pay below £139 per week to avoid NI.

56.   Deferring tax on your bonus

Problem

You want to extract funds from your company in such a way that you can save the business some tax but, at the same time, reduce your own self-assessment tax bill. But paying yourself a larger bonus will trigger tax and NI charges.

Tax and your salary

Money you take from your company as salary etc. will lower its profit but this is balanced by an opposite and equal increase in your income, which, of course, comes with a tax bill.

Usual solution - dividends

Usually it's more tax efficient for your company to pay you dividends rather than salary or a bonus. Although your company won't get a Corporation Tax (CT) deduction for dividends, the personal tax and NI savings recorded between you and your company will outweigh this. But sometimes paying dividends isn't an option. For example, they can only be paid out of profits and so dividends aren't an option if there are insufficient funds. In this situation a bonus is the practical choice and fortunately there is a way to defer the PAYE on this type of payment.

Tax and NI on bonuses

Where you pay a bonus to a director or employee, the tax and NI is payable under the PAYE system by the 19th of the following month. But your company doesn't have to actually pay the bonus to get a CT deduction for it, it just has to include it as an expense in its accounts and then actually pay it within nine months after the end of the accounting period. In other words, your company is able to get a tax deduction but defer paying PAYE tax and NI on your bonus as long as you don't draw the money.

Tax and NI on salary

Tax and NI deferral works for bonuses but it can work equally well for salaries. So as long as you can personally do without some of your regular salary, you can use the same strategy to defer PAYE by replacing salary with a regular once a year bonus.

Example

Acom Ltd pays each of its four directors a salary of £90,000 per year. But instead of paying it equally over twelve months it agrees that for the year ended December 31 2012 it will pay £5,000 a month as salary and the rest as a bonus at a time approved by the board. In September 2013 the directors approve payment of the £30,000 bonus (£2,500 x twelve months) and the PAYE for this is payable on October 19 2013. Acom will get a CT deduction for the bonus in its 2012 accounts even though payment has been deferred. The table below shows how much PAYE tax and NI can be postponed by Acom by deferring just the January 2012 salary:

	£
Directors' PAYE tax deferred on £2,500 at 40%	1,200
Directors' NI deferred on £2,500 at 2%	50
Acom's NI deferred on £2,500 at 13.8%	345
Total tax and NI deferred for each director	1,595
Four directors – total PAYE deferred	6,380

Trap. The Taxman has strict rules about when a bonus is treated as paid and the PAYE payable. It's vital that if you want this tax deferral plan to work, the bonus is beyond the reach of the director or employee in question until the time is right. When the board agrees the bonus make a minute in the company records which says that the director or employee can't draw the money until payment is approved. Make sure it's approved within nine months from the end of the company's accounting year to ensure the earliest CT deduction.

Download Zone

For a **Sample Board Minute**, visit **http://books.indicator.co.uk**. You'll find the access code on page 2 of this book.

Solution

Deferring payment of bonuses until nine months after the company's financial year can defer PAYE by up to 21 months without delaying the tax relief for the company. Replace regular salary with bonuses to make best use of this tax break. Record a board minute saying that the bonus won't be paid until approved by the board.

57. Dividend waiver

Problem

When a company pays a dividend all the shareholders receive a payment in proportion to their shareholding. Shareholders who pay tax at the basic rate won't have anything more to pay, but if you're liable at the higher rates, there's an additional income tax charge.

Classic solution

Dividend waivers are often used for planning purposes. Broadly, it involves a shareholder waiving their entitlement to the dividend before the right to it has accrued. A dividend waiver can therefore be used as a method of reducing the income a shareholder receives from the company.

Download Zone

For a free sample **Dividend Waiver**, visit **http://books.indicator.co.uk**. You'll find the access code on page 2 of this book.

Income diversion

Another possible use of a dividend waiver would be to divert income to one or more of the other shareholders.

Example

Trusty Ltd has an issued share capital of 100 ordinary shares; 50% of which are owned by Mr D and 50% by Mrs D. At March 31 2011 the company has distributable profits of £10,000. Mrs D is a basic rate (20%) taxpayer whereas Mr D's other sources of income mean that he pays tax at the rate of 42.5% on any additional dividends he receives from the company.

Scenario 1. The company declares a dividend of £150 per share in the knowledge that Mr D is going to waive his dividend and believes the position to be as set out in the table below.

DIVIDEND DECLARED	SCENARIO 1: £150 PER SHARE	
	£	£
Distributable reserves		10,000
Less dividend declared	(15,000)	
Add amount waived (50%)	5,000	
Dividend paid		(10,000)
Retained profits		-

Result. Mrs D gets her share plus Mr D's share of the company's profits but has no further tax to pay on the dividend.

Problem with diversion

If spotted, the Taxman could challenge this diversion of income on the basis that it constitutes a settlement for income tax purposes, which means the income would be deemed still to be Mr D's when calculating his tax bill. He will see that the waiver was integral in this arrangement as without it the total dividends would have exceeded available funds to distribute.

Solution

If a dividend of £100 per share is declared instead and Mr D waives his entitlement before the right to the dividend accrues, there is no bounty.

Dividend declared	Scenario 2: £100 per share	
	£	£
Distributable reserves		10,000
Less dividend declared	(10,000)	
Add amount waived (50%)	5,000	
Dividend paid		(5,000)
Retained profits		5,000

58. Making the right move to save tax

10

Problem

Where your taxable income is greater than £150,000 per annum, you'll be taxed at 50% on the excess. The general view of tax experts is therefore that you should aim to shift some income to your spouse or partner where they pay tax at a lower rate. But actually, you can be hit by tax rates of up to 60% where your income is substantially less.

What's the highest rate of tax?

If you take a look at the Taxman's published information, you would assume that 50% is the top rate of tax and that it only applied to those earning £150,000 or more. Actually, there is an effective rate of tax of 60% for those with incomes of between £100,000 and £116,210. The Taxman achieves this by withdrawing your tax-free allowances by £1 for every £2 your total income exceeds £100,000. The rate gradually drops back to around 45% on income of between £116,210 and £150,000.

> **TIP**
>
> If your total income is likely to exceed £100,000, then it's worthwhile considering income shifting.

Make a gift

The obvious choice is to make a gift of income-producing assets to your spouse, civil partner or unmarried partner. That way you ought to still benefit indirectly from the income produced.

Trap 1. There's no point in jumping out of the frying pan into the fire. So if your spouse etc. also has income of £100,000 or more, shifting some of yours to them isn't going to help!

Trap 2. Don't shift assets to your offspring to save income tax. If under 18, unless they're married, special anti-avoidance rules mean that any income the assets produce will still be treated as yours for tax purposes.

Which assets

Although you can save higher rate tax charges whatever income you shift, the decision on precisely which assets to transfer depends on your spouse's level of income. If it's less than their personal tax-free allowance, £8,105 for 2012/13, then certain types of income produce greater tax savings than others.

Trap. If your partner's income is £8,105 or less, don't transfer shares as the tax treated as paid on dividends is not refundable. This principle also applies to unit and investment trust distributions and dividends from foreign companies.

TIP

Aim to give other types of investment that either have no tax or basic rate tax deducted from the income they generate. Typically, this will be bank accounts and government, and other company, stocks and bonds. Your partner can claim a refund of the tax paid at source. Transferring property from which rental income is received will also reduce your joint liabilities.

Solution

Where your income exceeds £100,000, save tax at 60% by shifting some to your spouse or partner. If their income is less than £8,105, transfer assets paying interest, but not dividends, as tax already paid can't be reclaimed on these.

10

59. Taking regular dividends

Problem

Dividends can only be paid out of company profits. But you won't know how much profit your company made until the year has ended. If you want to take regular dividends during the year, how do you work out how much you can take?

Dividends only

An annual dividend rather than an annual bonus can save you tax and NI. Generally, this is the case when your company pays the lower rate of Corporation Tax on its profits, i.e. where these are no more than £300,000 for a year. The saving is due to the fact that NI is not payable either by you or your company on dividends.

NI reason

If there is no "salary", there is no NI payable and this will affect the entitlement to a range of state benefits such as retirement pension, Statutory Sick Pay etc. But this may not be an issue if other steps are being taken to provide coverage, e.g. a personal pension. Other rules, however, may lead you to pay a certain level of salary as well as a dividend.

NMW point

If you, as a director, have a contract of service, then the company would need to pay you a salary at least equal to the National Minimum Wage (NMW) level of £6.08 (£6.19 from October 1 2012) per hour. If this amount had to be paid anyway, then the NI issue is already covered.

Pension-related issue

From April 2011 there's a maximum limit of £50,000 that can be paid into your pension scheme each year. This is subject to a lifetime limit, which means you could play catch-up later.

Classic advice

You can pay a dividend monthly rather than quarterly or annually. The only requirement in setting the level of monthly dividend is that it must not be "illegal", i.e. exceed the company's distributable reserves. Distributable reserves represent the company's accumulated realised profits less its accumulated realised losses.

Trap. Following on from this the Taxman can contend that an illegal dividend is, for tax purposes, a loan to a shareholder and subject to a 25% tax charge on your company.

TIP

Look to pay this year's monthly dividend at a level not exceeding last year's distributable reserves, provided you are not making a loss in the current one. If you have quarterly accounts figures, this will assist you in monitoring the situation.

TIP

You can calculate the available profits for dividend (out of the current year) by dividing it by 0.80 (20% Corporation Tax rate), e.g. £40,000 dividend divided by 0.80 = £50,000 profits.

Paperwork

The dividend should be approved by a formal board minute, a profits available spreadsheet and a dividend voucher for each month.

Solution

You can make monthly dividend payments to yourself at a level not exceeding last year's distributable reserves, i.e. profit left in the company. But make sure you have all your paperwork in place to back up your calculation.

60. Justification for spouse's salary

Remuneration

Problem

Where you employ family members in your business, the amount you pay them often attracts a great deal of scrutiny from the Taxman, and he may refuse a tax deduction for all of it.

Equality of pay

The Taxman's view is that where your company employs your spouse or partner, they should be paid the same amount as you would pay any other person doing the same job. Anything higher may be deemed excessive and disallowed for tax as not being "wholly and exclusively" for the purposes of your trade.

Standard justification for rate of pay

Earnings of £11,700 per annum works out at just over 37 hours a week at the National Minimum Wage (NMW) of £6.08 (£6.19 from October 1 2012) per hour, over 52 weeks. However, the rate per hour that your spouse could earn might actually be higher than this. If you find out that the rate per hour an agency would charge to provide cover for your spouse's duties, then the Taxman would find it difficult to argue against this level of income being paid. Even after knocking off a percentage for the agency's profit margin, you'll end up with a rate higher than the NMW. For example, a rate of £8.35 an hour would justify an £11,700 package for only 27 hours work a week.

Improving the rate of pay

Let's take the case of a painter and decorator who employs his wife to assist him with admin, including taking calls from potential customers and actively advertising the business by word of mouth. It's reasonable to say that she is entitled to a commission on every new client she introduces to the business. And that can be commission worked out as a percentage of the value of the job.

TIP

Calculate commission due to your spouse based on the work or clients introduced by them to your company. This will help justify any regular payment they receive from the company. Have different commission rates for different products or services.

The important point is that whatever you do, document and log everything. Keep a spreadsheet of how the commission is calculated and has been built up. The Taxman then has to look at your business on the facts unique to it. He then can't rely on his long list of case law to please himself and declare what has been paid to your spouse as being excessive and not related to the trade.

Download Zone

For a **Spouse's Job Description**, visit **http://books.indicator.co.uk**. You'll find the access code on page 2 of this book.

Solution

As well as paying a basic salary to your spouse or partner for general administrative assistance to your business, pay them a commission for any work they introduce. This will be difficult for the Taxman to challenge.

61. A tax-effective salary waiver

Problem

Let's say you currently take a salary of £90,000 from your company but for tax reasons you want to reduce this to £7,225 for 2012/13. At this level you'll pay no tax or NI. Could this radical change trigger an enquiry from the Taxman?

Possible enquiries

The Taxman's view in cases where directors have previously enjoyed a large salary but now take a small one plus a dividend is not entirely clear. There is anecdotal evidence that the Taxman's Compliance Office Teams are seeking to treat some such dividends as if they were salary - meaning more income tax and NI payable, but this doesn't happen in every case.

What can you do?

Call it a fee not a salary. How does this help? The argument goes like this. Directors are appointed office holders under the **Companies Act** and they may perform extensive duties for the company in this capacity. Their remuneration for this is by way of a fee, the level of which may be determined from time to time and is normally approved by the members of the company at the Annual General Meeting. In such a case, there is no reason why the level of the fee should not be set at, say, £40,000 last year but only £7,225 this year. Such fees are still employment earnings subject to deductions of tax under PAYE and NI.

Minimum wage problem

Some directors have a separate employment contract. The terms of such a contract will include the payment of a salary, usually agreed in advance. Where an employment contract exists, the employer cannot unilaterally alter the terms of it.

The director without a contract of employment is not a worker for the purposes of the National Minimum Wage legislation. However, a director who is a worker, i.e. has an employment contract, must be paid at least the NMW rates of £6.08 (£6.19 from October 1 2012) per hour for a 37-hour week for 52 weeks a year, yielding a salary of around £11,700. Therefore, a reduction in salary to £7,225 isn't possible.

Husband and wife companies

The Taxman is trying to get the dividends in husband and wife companies taxed as the sole income of the main earner. This is in the absence of them taking a reasonable salary from the company. So by reducing your salary you could open yourself up to future attack.

Salary waiver

A better alternative is that you waive part of your salary. That is, formally give up the right to receive it in advance of it being paid to you. You can vary the amount of salary you waive from year to year.

What does a salary waiver entail? The Taxman takes the view that entitlement to salary accrues on a daily basis. Therefore, the waiver of remuneration must take place before the earliest event causes it to be treated as taxable. If this is the case, the Taxman can't successfully argue that any subsequent amount, e.g. a dividend, is remuneration.

Trap. For a salary waiver to be valid, it must be properly recorded and carried out. Some form of written documentation is therefore essential. A letter from you to the company stating your intention should suffice.

Download Zone

For a **Salary Waiver**, visit **http://books.indicator.co.uk**. You'll find the access code on page 2 of this book.

Solution

To reduce the risk of a tax enquiry, where you reduce your salary dramatically and take dividends instead, keep a properly executed salary waiver on record.

62. Salary sacrifice for tax-free subsistence

Problem

Your sales are down while related admin costs are up, so you're looking for ways to cut costs. How can you do this while rewarding staff at the same time?

Staff travel expenses

Your sales force need to eat while out on the road chasing those elusive deals, and you allow them to claim reasonable expenses for meals if they provide receipts. Processing all those expenses claims is very time-consuming. So in place of receipted meals you could pay a scale rate for daily subsistence costs in line with the Taxman's benchmark rates. (For details of these see the Appendix.)

Scale rates for meals

The Taxman's rates of £5 per daytime meal, or £15 for an evening meal, look pretty mean. However, these amounts are free of tax and NI. So to receive the equivalent amount in their pockets your staff would need gross pay of £7.25 per meal, assuming they're liable to basic rate tax. Over a year this could be the equivalent to pay of £1,667.50 for one meal per working day (230 days per year excluding holidays), or £3,565 for two daytime meals per working day. Once you point this out to your staff they may agree to reduce their gross pay to receive the full tax-free meal allowance.

Salary sacrifice

Reducing gross pay in return for a tax-free benefit is known as a salary sacrifice. The Taxman is happy for you to use such tax-saving allowances, but you must reach an agreement with your staff before reducing the pay they are entitled to. You'll also need to record their new level of gross pay as an amendment to their employment contract.

Trap. Where your staff are paid only just above the National Minimum Wage rate, you must not reduce their pay below that level, even if the difference is made up with the tax-free meal allowance. This is because the meal allowance doesn't count as part of the National Minimum Wage rate.

Tax savings

By reducing an employee's gross pay by the two meals per day allowance of £10, each member of staff will see an increase in their annual take home pay of £736. You could also benefit from this by sharing these savings with your employees. Do this by reducing their gross pay by an amount equal to half the daily allowance, but still pay the full £10 per day as a meal allowance. This will cost you £991 per year, which will give each employee an increase in net pay of £1,518 per year (see the Appendix for details of how this is calculated).

Admin savings

If you use the Taxman's benchmark rates for meal allowances, you avoid the need to process hundreds of expense claims from your staff, and you don't have to record the expenses on a Form P11D for each employee. However, you must agree this arrangement in advance with the Taxman, otherwise he won't let you off completing the P11D forms.

Trap. The Taxman is not inclined to agree to a salary sacrifice arrangement where you intend to pay meal allowances at more than his benchmark rates.

Solution

Use subsistence expenses as a salary sacrifice to provide a tax-free pay rise for your employees. This could increase their net pay by up to £713 per year whilst reducing your admin burden.

SECTION 11

Appendices

Weblinks

Tax breaks for environmentally friendly cars

http://www.greencarsite.co.uk/

http://www.low-co2-cars.co.uk/

http://www.thegreencarwebsite.co.uk

Using capital losses against your income tax bill

http://www.hmrc.gov.uk/helpsheets/hs286.pdf

Deferring the CGT bill on shares

http://www.hmrc.gov.uk/helpsheets/hs295.pdf

Company share buy back

http://www.hmrc.gov.uk/cap/#17

Different accounting and tax treatment for expenses

http://www.hmrc.gov.uk/manuals/bimmanual/bim31115.htm

Reducing the tax cost of selling a company

http://www.hmrc.gov.uk/manuals/cgmanual/CG46805.htm

Advance expenses for contractors

http://www.hmrc.gov.uk/helpsheets/490.pdf

Income Protection Insurance

http://www.hmrc.gov.uk/manuals/eimanual/EIM06410.htm

Personal use of company assets

http://www.hmrc.gov.uk/manuals/eimanual/eim21631.htm

http://www.hmrc.gov.uk/manuals/eimanual/eim21200.htm

Making a profit from Gift Aid

Oxfam "Tag and Bag" scheme:

http://www.oxfam.org.uk/tagyourbag

British Heart Foundation shops:

http://www.bhf.org.uk/get-involved/donate/gift-aid.aspx

The PDSA retail scheme:

http://www.pdsa.org.uk/how-you-can-help/gift-aid

Shift income without shifting the asset

http://www.hmrc.gov.uk/forms/form17.pdf

Arrears of pension contributions

http://www.hmrc.gov.uk/manuals/bimmanual/bim46035.htm

Transferring property as pension premiums

Suffolk Life:

http://www.suffolklife.co.uk/HOME/PUBLIC/PSPROPERTY/page213843.asp

Prudential:

http://www.pru.co.uk/contact_us/

James Hay:

http://www.jameshay.co.uk/Investments/CommercialProperty.aspx

Making use of personal losses in a company

http://www.hmrc.gov.uk/helpsheets/hs227.pdf

Tax relief for your personal helper

http://www.hmrc.gov.uk/manuals/eimanual/EIM32415.htm

Selling a car to your company

	£	ANNUAL TAX/NI COST (£)
Details of car		
List price of car	10,000	
CO_2 emissions, say	149	
Taxable benefit (20% of list price)	2,000	
Tax and NI charges for company car		
Tax for director/employee at 40% (maximum)	800	
Or		
Tax for director/employee at 20%	400	
Class 1A NI for company at 13.8% of taxable benefit	276	
Total tax and NI cost of company car (higher rate taxpayer)		1,076
Or		
Total tax and NI cost of company car (basic rate taxpayer)		676
		Annual tax relief
Company's tax position		
Cost of car to company	8,000	
Residual value in, say, 3 years	3,000	
Capital allowances	5,000	
Corporation Tax relief at 20% (small profits rate)		1,000
Or		
Corporation Tax relief at 26% (main rate)		1,200
Average annual capital allowances:		
Corporation Tax relief at 20% (small profits rate)		333
Or		
Corporation Tax relief at 24% (main rate)		400

	£	ANNUAL TAX/NI COST (£)
Running costs:		
Insurance and breakdown cover	390	
Servicing/maintenance etc. - average over three years (see note)	550	
Finance/parking permit/minor repairs etc., say	320	
Vehicle Excise Duty (road tax)	110	
Class 1A NI	207	
Total annual running costs	1,577	
Corporation Tax relief at 20% (small profits rate)		316
Or		
Corporation Tax relief at 24% (main rate)		378
Total Tax relief claimed by company (small profits rate)		649
Or		
Total tax relief claimed by company (main rate)		778
Note:		
Annual service		
Tyres (6 x £80 over 3 years)		
Cleaning etc.		

Gift of a holiday home

Conditions for special tax treatment of furnished holiday letting property (FHLP)

The long-standing rule that says to qualify as an FHLP a property must not be let out for periods of more than 30 days at a time remains unchanged. But the minimum number of days it must be rented out during a twelve-month period has been increased.

The property must be:

- rented out commercially, i.e. not just letting your friend use it for a free break, for 105 days (the previous rule was 70 days); and
- available for letting for 210 days (previously 140 days).

There's a loophole in the new rules which means that you can stick with the old letting limits for up to two years. However, this won't be given automatically, you'll have to make an election.

Election

You can continue to use the existing "number of days" letting rule by writing to the Taxman and requesting that this should apply. No special wording or form is required but this election must be made within two years of the end of the tax years for which you want it to apply.

CGT planning with children

Example

CAPITAL GAINS TAX			
Planning using children's annual exemption			
Information and assumptions for calculations:			
	£		£
Property purchased in 1990 for:			90,000
Property market value in May 2012			190,000
Increase in value (capital gain)			100,000
Gift in May 2012			
One tenth share to child A - Market value	17,000	see note	
Gift after April 5 2013			
One tenth share to child B - Market value	17,000	see note	
Sale in March 2014			
Net proceeds after costs, e.g. legal and agents fees	295,000		
Capital Gains Tax computations:			
On each gift to the children:			
Market value of property gifted - see above			17,000
Less:			
Cost of property (one tenth of the total)			9,000
Chargeable capital gain			8,000
Less: Annual exemption			10,600
Gain subject to tax			Nil
On the sale of the property in 2014:			
Each child's share			29,500
Less: Cost at time of gift			17,000
Chargeable capital gain			12,500
Less annual exemption for 2014/15 estimate at, say,			10,600
Gain liable to tax			1,900
By transferring a one tenth share of the property to two children annual exemptions have sheltered gains as follows:			
Parents annual exemptions used on gifts (£8,000 x 2)			16,000
Children's annual exemptions on final sale (£10,600 x 2)			21,200
Total			37,200
Tax saved (£37,200 x 28%)			10,416
Note. Although mathematically a tenth share of the property value is £19,000, a discount of around 10% must be used to value a minority share.			

Mileage allowances for contractors

HMRC approved mileage rates

Car. Approved rates for employees using their own cars for business are 45p per mile for the first 10,000 miles and 25p per mile thereafter. For motorcycles the rate is 24p per mile and for bikes, 20p per mile.

Fuel. Advisory rates for employee private mileage reimbursement or employer reimbursement of business miles (old rates in brackets).

ENGINE SIZE	PETROL	DIESEL	LPG
Up to 1,400cc/1,600cc Diesel	15p (14p)	12p (13p)	11p (10p)
1,401(1,601)/2,000cc	18p (16p)	15p (13p)	13p (12p)
Over 2,000cc	26p (23p)	18p (16p)	19p (18p)

Full calculation of figures used in the example

Van running costs	
Cost of van	£4,500
Value after three years	£750
Total depreciation	£3,750
Depreciation averaged over three years	£1,250
Servicing	£450
Tyres and sundries (average per year)	£160
Insurance	£300
Vehicle excise duty (road tax)	£140
Sub total	£2,300
Private use adjustment 20%	(£460)
Tax allowable costs	£1,840
Fuel costs on 14,000 business miles	£1,550
Total tax allowable costs	£3,390
Compared with:	
Mileage allowance	
First 10,000 miles at 45p	£4,500
Additional miles at 25p	£1,000
Total tax allowable mileage claim	£5,500
Less:	
Extra tax relief achieved	£1,610
Extra tax relief at 20%	£322
Extra Class 4 NI relief at 9%	£145
Total annual tax and NI saving	£451
Over three years	£1,353

A DIY IHT loan plan

Recommended terms and conditions to include in a loan

When making a personal loan to a family member for the purpose of freezing the value of part of your estate you should always have a written loan agreement. It might be wise to lodge a copy of this with the person or firm that holds your will. This will ensure that there's third party corroboration should the Taxman try to challenge the existence of the loan.

The loan should be open ended, in other words there is no set repayment date. Instead, the agreement should include a clause which allows you to demand full repayment with, say 60 days' notice.

The idea of making the loan to your relative is for them to invest the money and take the income and gains generated. However, you might want to make it a condition of the loan that you have to approve of the investments before they are made or changed. This will give you some protection against the possibility of the borrower blowing the money and not being able to repay the loan if you need it.

Making a profit from Gift Aid

Calculation showing the 60% tax rate

60% tax rate

The Taxman's budget notes say that 50% will be the top rate of tax with effect from April 6 2010, and that it will apply only to those with taxable income of £150,000 or more. But actually the effective rate of tax of 60% for those with incomes between £100,000 and £116,210 (approximately). This higher than published rate is achieved by the Taxman through the withdrawal of the personal tax-free allowance at the rate of £1 for every £2 your total income exceeds £100,000. The examples below show how this will work in practice.

EXAMPLE 1			£		£	
Earnings			100,000			
Tax-free allowance			6,475			
Taxable income			93,525			
Chargeable at	20%		37,400	=	7,480	
Chargeable at	40%		56,125	=	22,450	
Total tax due on £100,000					29,930	
EXAMPLE 2						
But if earnings were, say,			110,000			
Tax-free allowances		6,475				
But these will be reduced by £1 for every £2 earnings exceed £100,000						
Excess income £10,000, therefore		(5,000)				
Allowances reduced by £5,000			1,475			
Taxable income			108,525			
Chargeable at	20%		37,400	=	7,480	
Chargeable at	40%		71,125	=	28,450	
Total tax due on £110,000					35,930	
The extra tax on the additional £10,000 earnings is					6,000	i.e. 60%

EIS carry-back restrictions scrapped

Tax on capital gains which you make from selling or transferring assets can be deferred indefinitely, where the asset in question was sold or transferred within the 36 months before you invest in the Enterprise Investment Scheme (EIS), or within the twelve months after it.

Example

If you were to make a capital gain on selling some shares of, say, £50,000, in 2011/12, and later, say, in 2014/15, invested £30,000 into an EIS, then £30,000 of the tax payable on the earlier gain could be deferred from charge. If you had already paid tax on the gain, then you would receive a refund of this.

Deferral relief is unlimited, unlike the income tax relief which on applies to investments in EISs up to £500,000 per annum. Importantly, it can be claimed by investors (individuals or trustees) whose interest in the company exceeds 30%.

Transferring assets to your pension fund

More information on SIPPs

SIPP stands for "self-invested personal pensions". They are a "do-it-yourself" form of pension that gives much greater control to the policyholder rather than a pension company and allows an individual to make their own choice of investments within certain restrictions laid down by the government.

Anyone taking out a SIPP must be a UK resident and under 75.

In specie transfers

Since April 6 2006 there is only one set of rules governing the permitted investments for all registered pension schemes, i.e. SIPPs and small self-administered pension schemes (SASS) (see below). In brief, the following types of investment may be transferred as in specie contributions into a pension fund:

- commercial property in the UK or located overseas

- hotels, guest houses and nursing homes

- riding stables and golf courses

- forestry, woodland and agricultural land

- non-income producing land

- shares in unrelated companies, including:

    - Venture Capital Trust shares
    - Enterprise Investment Scheme shares
    - shares acquired from employee share schemes
    - shares in Real Estate Investment Trusts (REITS).

Shares held as investments do not have to be quoted, but unquoted shares must be valued on a fair market value basis before transfer.

A SASS can hold up to 5% of its fund value in shares of the sponsoring employer or an associated company, or up to 20% of the fund where the shares relate to more than one sponsoring employer. A SIPP can hold up to 100% of its fund in the shares of the employer of the scheme members, but not where that company has established a trust to run the SIPP, as that would make the pension scheme an occupational scheme.

Using your company as your pension fund

Example

JOHN'S BUSINESS	£
Sale proceeds from J Ltd shares July 2012	818,280
Less cost of shares	(100)
Chargeable gain	818,180
Less annual Capital Gains Tax exemption	(10,600)
Net chargeable gain	807,580
Tax due at entrepreneurs' rate 10%	80,758
Taking a dividend	
Company's net reserves taken as dividend	818,180
Add tax credit at nine-tenths of dividend	90,909
Less 2012/13 basic rate band	(37,370)
Chargeable to income tax at higher rate	874,719
Additional rate tax at 42.5%	371,756
Less tax credit	(90,909)
Net additional tax due	280,847
Spreading the dividends	
Tax-free allowances 2011/12	8,105
Basic rate band	34,370
Total	42,475
Deduct John's income other than dividends from J Ltd	(15,000)
Maximum amount of gross dividends that John can take without further tax	24,475
Less tax credit	(2,748)
Actual amount John can take from company without paying higher rate tax	24,728

Repaying share capital

From October 1 2008, a private company can reduce its issued capital by special resolution supported by a solvency statement. This is a new process of capital reduction under the Companies Act 2006 and is only applicable to private companies. A company must deliver to Companies House:

- a copy of a special resolution authorising the capital reduction
- a copy of the solvency statement made in accordance with sections 642(1)(a) and 643 Companies Act 2006
- a memorandum of capital
- a statement of compliance by the directors.

All the company directors must sign the solvency statement. This is a statement confirming that each director has formed the opinion that:

- at the date of the statement there are no grounds on which the company could be found to be unable to pay its debts; and
- if it is intended to commence a winding-up at any time in the twelve months following the statement, the company will be able to pay its debts within twelve months of the commencement of the winding up; and in any other case, the company will be able to pay its debts within the year following the date of the solvency statement.

The company must send or make available at a general meeting (depending on whether the resolution is proposed as a written resolution or at general meeting) a copy of the solvency statement to every eligible member of the company.

A memorandum of capital is a breakdown of the company's share capital structure following the reduction.

A statement of compliance by the directors is confirmation that the company made a copy of the solvency statement available to each of the eligible members as required and that the solvency statement was not made more than 15 days before the company's members passed the resolution.

You must send a copy of the solvency statement and resolution, and the memorandum of capital and statement of compliance by the directors, to Companies House. All of the documents should be sent to Companies House within 15 days of the passing of the resolution. Wherever possible, you should send all the forms together. In any event, the reduction of capital will not take effect until Companies House has registered a copy of the solvency statement, resolution and memorandum of capital.

Companies House has not prescribed forms for this process and you will have to produce your own documents. For further information and detail on the content of these documents, please follow the link below to the legislation:

http://www.legislation.gov.uk/uksi/2008/1915/made

Salary sacrifice for tax-free subsistence

Subsistence expenses example

MEAL ALLOWANCE		ONE MEAL	TWO MEALS
Working days	5 days x 46 working weeks	£230.00	£230.00
Daily meal allowance	£5 for each meal	£5.00	£10.00
Total meal allowance		£1,150.00	£2,300.00

Option 1 - Full salary sacrifice

			ONE MEAL RATE		TWO MEAL RATE	
			£	£	£	£
			Before sacrifice	With sacrifice for allowance	Before sacrifice	With sacrifice for allowance
Gross pay		A	25,000.00	23,850.00	25,000.00	22,700.00
Tax free pay (personal allowance)		B	7,475.00	7,475.00	7,475.00	7,475.00
Meal allowance (see above)		C	-	1,150.00	-	2,300.00
Tax due for basic rate payer	A-B+Cx20%	D	3,505.00	3,275.00	3,505.00	3,045.00
NI earnings threshold		F	7,228.00	7,228.00	7,228.00	7,228.00
Employees' NI	A-Fx12%	G	2,132.64	1,994.64	2,132.64	1,856.64
Net pay including allowance	A-D-G	H	19,362.36	19,730.36	19,362.36	20,098.36
Net pay increase for employee:		I	£368.00		£736.00	

Appendices

			ONE MEAL RATE		TWO MEAL RATE	
			£	£	£	£
NI earnings threshold		F	7,072.00	7,072.00	7,072.00	7,072.00
Employers' NI	A-Fx13.8%	J	2,474.06	2,315.36	2,474.06	2,156.66
Total cost to employer	A+C+J		27,474.06	27,315.36	27,474.06	27,156.66
Employer savings		K	**£158.70**		**£317.40**	
Employer savings plus employee pay increase	I+K		**£526.70**		**£1,053.40**	

Option 2 - Half salary sacrifice (add allowance to gross pay and reduce by half)

			ONE MEAL RATE		TWO MEAL RATE	
			£	£	£	£
			Before sacrifice	With sacrifice for allowance	Before sacrifice	With sacrifice for allowance
Gross pay		A	25,000.00	24,425.00	25,000.00	23,850.00
Tax free pay (personal allowance)		B	7,475.00	7,475.00	7,475.00	7,475.00
Meal allowance (see above)		C	-	1,150.00	-	2,300.00
Tax due for basic rate payer	A-B+(Cx50%) x20%	D	3,505.00	3,390.00	3,505.00	3,275.00
NI earnings threshold		F	7,228.00	7,228.00	7,228.00	7,228.00
Employees' NI	A-Fx12%	G	2,314.20	2,245.20	2,314.20	2,176.20
Net pay including allowance	A-D-G	H	19,180.80	19,939.80	19,180.80	20,698.80
Net pay increase for employee:		I	**£759.00**		**£1,518.00**	

			ONE MEAL RATE		TWO MEAL RATE	
			£	£	£	£
NI earnings threshold		F	7,072.00	7,072.00	7,072.00	7,072.00
Employers' NI	A-Fx13.8%	J	2,474.06	2,394.71	2,474.06	2,315.36
Total cost to employer	A+C+J		27,474.06	27,969.71	27,474.06	28,465.36
Employer costs		K	£495.65		£991.30	
Employer costs less employee pay increase	I-K		£263.35		£526.70	

The tax and National Insurance-free benchmark subsistence rates

1. Breakfast rate (irregular early starters only) - up to £5.00, where the employee leaves home earlier than usual and before 6.00am and incurs a cost for breakfast taken away from home. However, where an employee has to leave home regularly before 6.00am because, for example, of working an early shift, a payment of a breakfast allowance won't qualify for tax and NI-free status.

2. One meal rate (five-hour rate) - up to £5.00, where the employee has been away from home or the normal place of work for a period of at least five hours and has incurred the cost of a meal.

3. Two meal rate (ten-hour rate) - up to £10.00, where the employee has been away from home or the normal place of work for a period of at least ten hours and has incurred the cost of one or more meals.

4. Evening meal rate (irregular late finishers only) - up to £15.00, where the employee has to work later than usual, finishes work after 8.00pm having worked the normal day and has to buy a meal which would usually have been taken at home.

If an allowance under the five or ten-hour rule is paid, the late meal allowance may also be paid where the employee finishes work after 8.00pm and buys a meal that would usually have been taken at home. However, if the employee regularly finishes work late, for example because they do shift work in the evening, the conditions for the late evening meal allowance won't qualify for tax and NI-free status.

Notes

Notes

Notes